Dedication

This book is dedicated to the men and women who perished on September 11, 2001. And to all of the men and women who are serving, or have proudly served, our country. God Bless America!

Foreword

Antique Limoges at Home expands Debby DuBay's unique focus on Limoges porcelain presented in her first book, *Living with Limoges*. By illustrating that Limoges, whether factory or American decorated, can be incorporated into the total décor of our homes, *Living with Limoges* served as an inspiration for collectors to see Limoges in a new dimension—to go beyond the acquisition of examples solely for a table setting, a specialized collection, or even an investment. Debby DuBay's new book continues that theme by showcasing more beautiful and interesting pieces which can be actively enjoyed daily rather than confined to holiday tables or only observed from a glass-fronted cabinet. The Victorians embraced this idea of "living" with fine porcelain. Many of the items collectors seek are from that era. From Debby DuBay's artistic presentation, it is obvious that lovely and unusual pieces of Limoges can and should be "lived with" today, gracing our homes as they had the homes of past generations. Additionally, Limoges jewelry was introduced in Ms. DuBay's first book under "Wearing Your Limoges." More examples in her new edition make it apparent that "living with Limoges" need not be limited to enhancing home decoration but can adorn you personally as well!

During the course of collecting and learning about a subject, some collectors find, as a result of their endeavors, that they are able to publish and add to the information about a subject. This has been the case with Debby DuBay. Collecting Limoges, as a hobby, prompted her to increase her collection. As her interest and collection grew, she established a business devoted to Limoges. Based on her experiences and research, she discovered that she could indeed contribute to collector knowledge. Now having completed two books about Limoges porcelain, Debby DuBay continues to be a collector and dealer of this fine china, but she has become an educator as well. I applaud her exemplary works which will certainly increase the interest in Limoges porcelain. Her books will delight and inform today's collectors—moreover, and importantly, these books will be appreciated as reference sources by future collectors through the years.

—Mary Frank Gaston

Considered the leading expert on porcelain, Mary Frank Gaston is a dealer, collector, appraiser, and author of twenty-one books on china and metals, including the *Collector's Encyclopedia of Limoges Porcelain*, *Third Edition*. The subjects of her other books include America Belleek, Art Deco, Blue Willow, Brass & Copper, Flow Blue, Haviland, and R.S. Prussia. Her latest book, *Collector's Encyclopedia of English China*, has just been released.

Acknowledgments

Sharing ideas with collectors and decorators on how to live and decorate with their Limoges porcelain was a unique concept for a collector's book. Professional photographer Linda LaBonte-Britt photographed thirty-plus homes from entryways to powder rooms, and Ann Spataro shot thousands of photographs of Limoges, including buttons and brooches. These photographs, along with a price guide, complete description of each piece, and a mark section were incorporated into a composition appropriately titled *Living with Limoges* (www.livingwithlimoges.com).

Peter Schiffer, Schiffer Publishing Company, embraced my idea and *Living with Limoges* was published. I sincerely thank Schiffer Publishing for allowing me to present this unique format to collectors and for publishing the first book on Limoges to include Limoges jewelry. Once again, Peter has allowed me to be creative in *Antique Limoges at Home* and has provided readers, collectors, and decorators with another fabulous book on Limoges art. I will be forever thankful to Peter for believing in me, and supporting my idea of providing collectors of Limoges a book in this unique format.

Writing a book is like having a child; the entire process is to be awed, the experience provides a lifetime of joy, and the pain and expense are forgotten upon its release. So much so, that you decide to have more, or in this case, write another! I sincerely thank my editor, Donna Baker and the entire professional Schiffer team. With a few suggestions from Donna, *Antique Limoges at Home* was conceived.

This book would not have been possible without the photography support of Linda LaBonte-Britt and the artistic ability of Ellie Smerlas. A talented artist, Ellie provided artist renditions of the marks that were unavailable to photograph in the Limoges, American Limoges, and Reproduction marks section.

Special recognition goes to my mentor, Mary Frank Gaston. I am honored and absolutely thrilled that she has provided the forward for *Antique Limoges at Home*.

I thank Pearl Dexter, Editor of *Tea A Magazine*, and Erika Kotite, Editor of *Victorian Homes*, for their lovely magazines and for allowing me to expose their readers to the world of collecting and decorating with Limoges.

I thank the Haviland Collectors Internationale Foundation (www.havilandcollectors.com) for a professional organization that provides so much information to Limoges collectors, and for allowing me to use the chart of Haviland marks and dates.

Sincere thanks to my colleagues: Raymonde Limoges, author of *American Limoges*, and the leading expert in this field, for her professional guidance and assistance in writing the section on American Limoges; and Faye Strumpf, author of *Limoges Boxes*.

Special thanks goes to the descendants of Mr. Valentin Heyerdahl, specifically his daughter Maudes's niece, Barbara M. Garofalo, who provided me with all of the information and photographs in reference to Mr. Heyerdahl and his association with the Haviland and GDA Limoges factories. Also to Mr. Joe Murray, who allowed me to photograph his family's American Limoges dinnerware.

Fond recognition goes to Linda Berube, Yummy Mummy Cookie Factory, Andover, Massachusetts (www.cookiefavors.com), who provided the cookie art in the photographs. And to Nancy Bautzmann of Bautzmann Studio, Tucson, Arizona, a talented artist who incorporated a teapot from my private collection into an original painting that was on the cover of the 2001 Autumn issue of *Tea A Magazine*. Nancy has allowed me to include the photograph in the teapot section of this book.

Sincere thanks to all of my clients, friends, and fellow collectors for allowing me to photograph their lovely homes and private collections and/or for providing me with slides: Dave and Annie Brooks, Bruce Guilmette, Allan Ward and their beloved cat Nicholas, Sue Mickey, Collette Otwell, Karen Jacobs and Dr. Matt Gold, Arielle and Josh Gold, Candy Gammal, Barbara and David Gilchrist, Nancy and Jim Greeley, Rosalie Hanson, Mary Kelleher, Linda Minsky, Ellie and Maggie Smerlas, Debbie and Sam Streiff, Dr. Paul and Mrs. Diane Tower, Carolyn Lindsay Johnson and Douglas M. Johnson. A special thanks for the contributions of my fellow collectors who did not want to be officially recognized.

To my family, dear friends, and my husband, Dan Quinn, for your support, friendship, love, and untiring patience. I love you all very much.

And lastly, to all of the patriots: men and women who are serving or have selflessly served our country, many who gave their lives, so that we may live in freedom in this truly great and beautiful country ~ The United States of America.

Disclaimer

The current values in this book should be only used as a guide. This book is by no means intended to set prices for a specific piece of Limoges. The values provide a price range indicating what a piece of the same blank, with similar decoration and in similar condition, has sold for in retail shops, at auction, and on websites. Collectors, decorators, art enthusiasts, and individuals who just "have to have" a particular piece may be the cause of a wide variation of price ranges across the country.

Contents

Introduction

There are many wonderful decorating books available on the market, from "how to" books by Charlotte Moss to historic books on decoration by Edith Wharton. But try as I might, I could not find a single book with ideas on how to decorate when a collection is involved. Collectors are a unique breed. They do not care about the rules of decorating as long as they can fit in one more piece that they just "had to have." Collectors purchase the house that will enhance their collection or make their current home fit their collection's needs. Collectors will line their collections up on a fireplace mantel or on the floor if there is no more room. We will line china cabinets along a wall or have them built in. Aware of this dilemma as a collector, dealer, and self-professed design consultant, I knew the need for such a book existed.

Writing my first book *Living With Limoges* (www.livingwithlimoges.com), was a wonderful experience. The joy of sharing decorating ideas with obsessed and passionate collectors, while incorporating my knowledge of Limoges and love for this fabulous art form, was very rewarding. But, I couldn't stop there. The same feeling I get as a collector overcame me: I wanted more, more, more! Thus, *Antique Limoges at Home* is the compilation of decorating ideas from the homes of collectors I have had the opportunity to meet over the past decade as the owner of Limoges Antiques Shop in Andover, Massachusetts (www.limogesantiques.com). Stunning, professional photographs show Limoges collections in entryways, living rooms, dining rooms, bedrooms, powder rooms, patios, and more.

Antique Limoges at Home also addresses common questions: the difference between Limoges and American Limoges, reproductions and their marks, and the differences between particular Limoges blanks and their intended uses. This book provides information on artists; includes a comprehensive alphabetical marks section on Limoges, American Limoges and reproductions; and has a section dedicated to buttons and brooches, those tiny works of art on porcelain. But, what makes this book unique are the decorating ideas from a collector's perspective. More, more, more—in a collector's mind, there is always room for MORE!

Part I

Limoges ~ Fine Porcelain

Since the publication of my first book, *Living With Limoges*, the most frequently asked question I receive either by phone or through our websites is: "What is the difference between "Limoges" and "American Limoges?" There is much confusion regarding the difference between Limoges, a fine hard paste porcelain produced in France, and American Limoges, a pottery produced in the United States. The Limoges porcelain produced in France since 1771 is a fine hard paste porcelain that is lightweight, vitreous, and translucent. Dinnerware was produced along with hand painted decorative pieces such as jardinières and punch bowls and pieces of art such as paintings on porcelain and plaques. These pieces were sold either decorated or as blanks in fine department stores or to china painting factories. In contrast, the product called American Limoges was produced in the United States between 1897 and 1957 and is earthenware: a soft paste pottery that is heavy, semi-vitreous, and darker in color. Dinnerware made out of American Limoges was produced, as well as souvenirs, calendar plates, tea sets, and children's dishes. Production of these pieces was intended to satisfy the masses of middle class Americans who could not afford to purchase fine porcelain dinnerware from Europe. Marketing consisted of theater giveaways, furniture store specials, and free premiums with purchases in drug and grocery stores.

Limoges ~ "The Finest Hard Paste Porcelain in the World"

Limoges has become the generic name of the hard paste porcelain that was produced during the eighteenth, nineteenth, and into the twentieth century in one of the many factories in Limoges, a region of France situated about 250 miles southwest of Paris in the Vienne valley. Limoges is considered the finest hard paste porcelain in the world because of three very distinct characteristics. First, the essential ingredients making up the content of Limoges porcelain are all natural ingredients: feldspar, quartz, and kaolin. Second, the intense firing process forms a glaze that cannot be penetrated and makes Limoges porcelain an exquisite form of translucent pottery. The glaze on an antique piece of Limoges over a hundred years old will show no signs of crackling or crazing and if it has not been broken, a piece will look as beautiful as the day it was produced. Third, an abundance of the most prestigious and skilled artisans in the world along with the French flair for design and artistic style set the standard for both Europeans and Americans to emulate. These French artisans created masterpieces out of everything from decorative pieces of art to essential objects for daily use. Today, some of the most important pieces created during this era are on display at the "Musee de la porcelaine de Limoges" in Limoges, France.

During the nineteenth century, there were approximately thirty-two factories and sixty-two decorating studios in the Limoges region of France, with the number of factories increasing to forty-eight by 1920. Each factory had its own porcelain and decorating marks; many factories used several different marks during their porcelain production years. A piece of Limoges will have a mark *under* the glaze which indicates the factory that produced the piece of porcelain and it may also have a mark *over* the glaze which identifies the factory that decorated the piece. Currently, there are more than four hundred known marks to identify factories that produced and decorated Limoges. One of the best known factories is the Haviland factory. Other examples are the Jean Pouyat (J.P.L.) and Tressemann & Vogt (T&V) factories. At the back of this book is an alphabetical factory mark listing that will help you identify pieces of Limoges produced and decorated in a factory from the region. (For further research on the Limoges factories, see Mary Frank Gaston's *Collector's Encyclopedia of Limoges Porcelain, Third Edition*.) Even if these marks do not include the word "Limoges," the pieces these factories produced are correctly identified as Limoges porcelain. Today, Limoges is still considered the Mecca for hard paste porcelain in France and there are about forty factories currently producing and exporting table china, dinnerware sets, and Limoges boxes.

Limoges blanks—that is, the shape of the piece of porcelain—came in all forms and sizes: dinnerware; decorative pieces such as chargers and plaques; chocolate, coffee. and teapots; jardinières and planters; lamps; paintings on porcelain; punch bowls; tankards; cider pitchers; and vases. These Limoges blanks were produced in the factories in France. The blanks were then decorated in one of the factories in France or exported to the United States. Once in America, the blanks were then sold to one of the professional decorating factories in the United States, to china painting schools, or to a department store for one of the many amateur artists of the era to purchase and hand paint.

I believe the confusion between Limoges and American Limoges begins at the turn of the twentieth century, when more than 25,000 professional and amateur American china painters were decorating these imported blanks. The confusion deepens when we throw in the Haviland family factories. Well known for their production of dinner and tableware, Haviland & Company were manufacturers of china in Limoges, France, and importers with offices in New York City, New York. David Haviland was very successful in securing a foothold in the American marketplace. It was actually David Haviland's success in the American porcelain market, between 1842 and 1855, that inspired other porcelain factories in the Limoges region to export their wares. David sent his son Theodore to the United States to handle marketing and distribution of their Limoges in America while his other son, Charles-Edward, remained at the factory in France. Theodore was incredibly good at marketing and by 1866 the Haviland factories in France could not keep up with the overwhelming amount of orders from the United States. It was at this time that other porcelain producers, including those in America, took advantage of the market. Theodore was deeply distressed over the fact that his customers might associate an inferior porcelain product with the "Haviland" name. In 1876, he suggested that the name "Haviland" be stamped on the bottom of all of their pieces. As a marketing idea to entice stores to sell Haviland porcelain, he also suggested they stamp the name of the shop in America that sold these pieces on the bottom as well. For example, Wanamaker's department store in Philadelphia was given their own import mark. This mark is over the glaze and was on all Haviland pieces that were sold in their store after 1876.

Theodore Haviland Limoges France Decorator Mark, Mark p, ca. 1903, with the Wanamaker's department store identification mark.

In 1879, upon the death of his father, Theodore returned to France. In 1893, after a sibling squabble between Theodore and Charles-Edward, Theodore established the Theodore Haviland Company. Theodore Haviland was known for his superb designs and the development of "porcelaine mousseline," a whiter thinner product. Theodore Haviland dinnerware became very popular and there was an overwhelming American market desire for his porcelain. Everyone in America wanted a set of Haviland. From 1906 to 1907, the American Potters Association worked hard at limiting European porcelain imports. Trying to establish a market foothold and ensure their own success in the market, the Association lobbied Congress to impose a ban on porcelain imports. The Association's success in imposing such a ban in 1907, followed by World War I (1914-1918), dramatically affected porcelain exporting for the next few years.

The demand for Haviland china plummeted during World War I and these difficult years were followed by Theodore's death in 1919. Upon his death,

Theodore's eldest son, William, became Chairman of the Board of the Theodore Haviland factory. A creative thinker with market savvy, William decided to open a factory in the United States in order to increase the marketability of Limoges in America. In 1936, he opened a factory in New Castle, Pennsylvania that operated until 1957. Due to World War II (1939-1945) and the Nazi occupation in France, however, William was unable to import kaolin from the Limoges region and was forced to use kaolin found in other regions. The porcelain produced during this era was heavier, did not have the translucent look, and was a softer paste. The pieces produced in the Haviland factory in the United States were marked "Theodore Haviland, Made in America" and are easily identifiable.

The Havilands were a family of porcelain makers. David's brother Robert had a son, Charles Field, who worked in the Haviland & Company factories for a few years before establishing his own porcelain decorating studio in France in 1868. The Charles Field Haviland factory marks (CFH) can be found from 1868 to 1881. In 1881, Charles Field retired and Gérard, Dufraisseix, and Morel took over his factory operations. They continued to use the Charles Field factory marks (CFH) but added their own initials "GDM" under the CFH mark. In 1890, Mr. Morel left the business and by 1900, Gérard and Dufraisseix had a new partner, Mr. Edgar Abbot. From 1900 to the present, the Charles Field underglaze factory mark was deleted and the Gérard, Dufraisseix, and Abbot marks (GDA) were used. However, the "CH FIELD HAVILAND" mark was used as the overglaze decorating mark until 1941.

It was in 1886 that a Mr. Valentin Heyerdahl began his life as an expert in china goods and his employment of sixteen years with the Charles Field Haviland China company. In our world today, Americans may lose site of the fact that we are indebted to many of the European countries for their enterprising sons and daughters. Valentin Heyerdahl was one of those enterprising men and the obscure facts that follow may have been lost forever if not for the sheer coincidence that in 2001 his daughter Maude's niece, Barbara M. Garofalo, visited my shop.

Born in 1870 in Bergen, Norway, Valentin Heyerdahl and his family made the trip from their home in Sweden to the "New World" of New York City when he was a mere youth of fifteen. One year later, he secured a position with the Haviland Company in New York City. Mr. Heyerdahl became one of the most trusted and important employees, later becoming sole agent for the Charles Field Haviland company. Mr. Heyerdahl's business involved his traveling every year to Europe in the interests of the American trade, in connection with the importation of fine wares and china from the famous Limoges factories in France. In 1902, he resigned from Haviland & Co., and subsequently was employed by the Gérard, Dufraisseix, and Abbot (GDA) company until his death in November 1907.

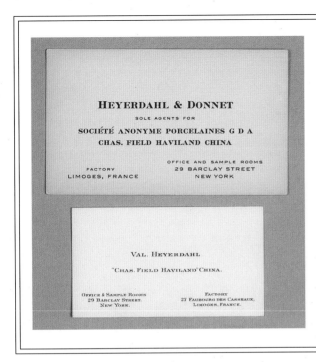

HEYERDAHL & DONNET
SOLE AGENTS FOR
SOCIÉTÉ ANONYME PORCELAINES G D A
CHAS. FIELD HAVILAND CHINA

FACTORY
LIMOGES, FRANCE

OFFICE AND SAMPLE ROOMS
29 BARCLAY STREET
NEW YORK

VAL. HEYERDAHL
"CHAS. FIELD HAVILAND" CHINA.

OFFICE & SAMPLE ROOMS
29 BARCLAY STREET,
NEW YORK.

FACTORY
27 FAUBOURG DES CASSEAUX,
LIMOGES, FRANCE.

Top: Mr. Valentin Heyerdahl's card from 1902-1907. He and his partner and friend, Mr. Donnet, were sole agents for the GDA Limoges Company. *Bottom*: Mr. Heyerdahl's card while employed with the Haviland China Company.

Photos of the GDA Factory, Limoges France, taken August 14, 1904.

The set of Limoges shown in these two photos is owned today by the family of Mr. Val Heyerdahl (his daughter's niece, Mrs. Barbara M. Garofalo). The dishes are marked under the glaze in green GDA over France, Gérard, Dufraisseix, and Abbot white ware Mark 1, ca. 1900-1941. They have an over the glaze decorating mark in green with gold letters GDA Limoges, Mark 4, ca. 1941. The covered serving dishes are marked with the Theodore Haviland Limoges France, Mark p, ca. 1903.

One of a pair of lovely centerpiece bowls/reticulated baskets made expressly for Mr. Val Heyerdahl as a Christmas gift in 1905. They are marked with the Gérard, Dufraisseix, and Morel Mark 3. The bowl is hand painted with rose buds and a center medallion of flowers by his wife Mrs. Ida E. Tobin, Mount Vernon, New York, a very proficient artist and china painter.

The bottom of the bowl.

For more detailed research on the Haviland factories, see *Celebrating 150 Years of Haviland China 1842-1992* by the Haviland Collectors Internationale Foundation and *Haviland China: The Age of Elegance* by Nora Travis (both listed in the bibliography). I also suggest joining the Haviland Collectors Internationale Foundation (P.O. Box 271383, Fort Collins, Colorado, 80527, or www.havilandcollectors.com).

American Limoges ~ *"Fashioned in America...for America"*

American Limoges is the name of the earthenware produced in the United States in Ohio from 1897 to 1957. This pottery was produced in several factories: The Ohio China Company, The Oliver China Pottery, and the Sterling China Factory. The Sterling China Factory was renamed Sebring China, which in turn was renamed the Limoges China Company. In the 1940s, the Limoges China Company added "American" to their title in order to distinguish their wares from the imported Limoges porcelain. The American Limoges China Company produced thousands of pieces of soft paste, creamy white, heavy chinaware. Other factories included Saxon Pottery, The Royal China Company, and The American Chinaware Corporation, an organized group of pottery manufacturers who joined forces.

Recognizing the need and desire of the average American family for a tableware that was stronger and less expensive than the tableware being imported from Europe, these factories imported English clay and combined chemical elements (as opposed to natural ingredients) to form the pottery known generically as "American Limoges." American Limoges is a semi-vitreous chinaware that is thick and durable. This type of earthenware will show signs of crazing and crackling on pieces less than fifty years old. Most American Limoges is decorated using the transfer ware process and is considered tableware rather than decorative pieces of art.

Table setting of an average American home from 1897 to 1957. The table is set with American Limoges, made in the United States. Rosalie pattern, Triumph Factory, ca. 1942-1949. This set was a wedding gift in 1943 to Joseph E. Murray, Sr. and his wife Gladys P. Murray. It is currently owned by their son, Joseph E. Murray, Jr. Complete 110-piece set: $175-$375.

One of the largest expenses in the production of tableware during the nineteenth and twentieth centuries was the decoration. Hand painting was tedious, costly, and not practical when trying to mass produce an inexpensive and everyday tableware. In England in the late 1700s, pottery decoration using a transfer had been introduced. In the 1800s, the French perfected this decorating technique, which they termed "decalcomania" (the French word for transfer decoration), and the process became widespread. Decalcomania became an inexpensive way of mass producing decorated tableware.

Decalcomania used a transfer process, resembling transfer colored papers, that when wet and pressed onto the porcelain transferred the design from the paper onto the piece. The American Limoges factories used this form of decorating by transfer ware almost exclusively. In the book *American Limoges* by Raymonde Limoges, in fact, only one hand painted piece is shown, a very rare vase. The savings from using transfer ware decoration and mass production of American Limoges dinnerware sets was passed directly onto the consumer. In 1943, for example, a 20-piece American Limoges dinnerware set in the National Bouquet pattern sold for $4.99. (Compare this price to a transfer ware decorated dinnerware set made of porcelain imported from Limoges France. A Haviland set would sell anywhere from $19.95 to $39.95, plus additional expense for a matching tea or coffee set, etc.) Practical, durable, and inexpensive, American Limoges dinnerware became an indispensable commodity in the average American home during the first half of the twentieth century.

American Limoges is a pottery that is decorated using "decalomania," a transfer process. This invention, used as a substitution for the slow hand painting method, was the largest factor in lowering the cost of chinaware. This set includes twelve 10-1/8" dinner plates, 7" plates, 6-3/8" plates, and 6" saucers with matching coffee cups.

This American Limoges set includes twelve 8-1/4" bowls, 6" bowls, 5-1/2" bowls, and a 9" vegetable bowl along with an oblong platter, a round platter, platter with handle, and gravy boat.

American Limoges covered soup tureen or bowl. $10-$20.

American Limoges sugar and creamer. Set: $12-$25.

American Limoges salt and pepper shakers. Set: $10-$15.

The mark or backstamp is the key to identification of a piece of American Limoges and there are just as many marks as factories. If the mark states any of the following or has these words in the mark, the piece was produced in the United States: Sebring Ohio, Made In U.S.A., American Limoges, Limoges China Co., American Limoges China Co., Made in U.S.A. LIMOGES, Warranted 22 K. Gold, U.S.A. 22 K. GOLD, Pleasantware Made in U.S.A. by Limoges, Union Made, TRIUMPH, Western Royal by Limoges-Sebring Associates, Sebring Limoges Associates, and MFG. BY AMERICAN Limoges.

A mark that states one of the following is most definitely a piece of American Limoges and is not a piece of Limoges produced in the Limoges region of France: Made in U.S.A., Sebring, Ohio, and American Limoges. For additional information refer to the American Limoges marks section at the back of this book. Those interested in further research should also see *American Limoges* by Raymonde Limoges.

Mark on the bottom of this 1943 American Limoges set of dinnerware. Note the words "Made in USA," allowing consumers to distinguish between this pottery and Limoges exported from France. Although not considered a piece of art, American Limoges can be fun to collect. Today, it is reasonable and durable—the same reasons it become desirable at the turn of the twentieth century.

In 1931, a lawsuit was filed by the City of Limoges Chamber of Commerce through the United States State Department contesting the use of the word "Limoges" on any porcelain produced outside of France. As a result of this lawsuit, it was determined that the Limoges name was a "restricted name" and protected by law. The Limoges name was to be used exclusively on porcelain pieces that contained clay from the Limoges region and that were produced in the factories in France. This clay containing kaolin or "white gold" is the major ingredient in fine hard paste porcelain. It was further determined that the use of the word "Limoges" on an earthenware product was misleading to the consumer and unfair to the factories in France that were producing high quality porcelains. In 1933, by the time the law was enacted, and by 1940, when there is the first documentation that the Limoges China Company added "American" to their name, it was too late to eliminate name association. Today, the association of the name "Limoges" with porcelain produced during the nineteenth and twentieth centuries in one of the factories from that region in France can cause confusion when a piece is found marked "American Limoges" or with any of the marks described above containing the word "Limoges."

Although collectible, American Limoges is not fine hard paste porcelain produced in the Limoges region in France and American Limoges items are not considered pieces of art. Keeping in mind this major difference, collecting American Limoges pottery can be a fun and rewarding endeavor.

Reproductions

In the 1970s, when I began collecting nineteenth century hand painted porcelain and decorative pieces of Limoges art, there were no Limoges reproductions. Come to think about it, the Vietnam War had not been officially declared over, women were just being integrated into traditional all-male career fields, computers took up entire rooms, and there was no Internet, e-commerce, websites, or eBay. Mary Frank Gaston had not written her first book on porcelain, Oprah was not a television icon, *Victoria Magazine* had not been established, Mark McGuire was a baby, and Nomar Garciapara had not even been born!

The 1970s found Americans traveling abroad and bringing back Limoges miniatures and other pieces as souvenirs. Richard Sonking had just begun a Limoges import business in New York City. (He is responsible for the resurgence of Limoges boxes, which did not gain popularity in America until the mid-1980s.) Individuals who could afford a Limoges dinnerware set imported from France could purchase one from Tiffany's, Gumps, or other fine department stores. In 1975, I fell in love with my first hand painted Limoges vase while serving in the military and visiting an antique shop in Paris, France. It was a large 14" tall vase with flamboyant handles and ethereal roses painted all around it. The painting was so vivid I swear you could smell the fragrance of the pink roses and feel the dew on their petals, and if you touched the stem, I was certain you would be pricked by the thorns. Smitten by the beauty of this exquisite art form, I purchased the vase for approximately $450—expensive at that time, but a great investment if I could only part with it. Today, a vase of this size and quality of painting is valued in the thousands of dollars. Antiquing in Europe in the 1970s was different from today and my fondest memories were finding complete sets of Limoges dinnerware at flea markets in France, Belgium, and England. Today, antiquing is a challenge; everyone is aware of the value of an antique. With the exposure, demand, and limited supply of nineteenth century Limoges porcelain, new opportunities have arisen for the unaware and unethical to pawn off an inferior or reproduction piece of china as a piece of Limoges.

When Mary Frank Gaston's first edition of the *Collector's Encyclopedia of Limoges* was published in 1980, there were virtually no reproductions or fakes on the market. With her second book's release in 1992, she informed the collector of reproductions being imported to the United States from Taiwan. By her third edition, the book had an entire section dedicated to "Fake and Misleading Limoges Marks." Websites and Internet auctions, along with just enough market exposure to entice the consumer, have contributed to a market overrun with reproduction pieces produced in Taiwan and sold as Limoges. Indeed, due to national exposure and increased popularity of decorative Limoges, reproductions are flooding the market.

Since the late 1990s, there has been an explosion in the popularity of Limoges. In 1997 and 1999, *Victoria Magazine* introduced their 4.1 million subscribers to Limoges porcelain. In 1999, Janet Allon and the editors of *Victoria Magazine* wrote a best selling book, *The Business of Bliss, How to Profit from Doing What You Love*, and dedicated an entire chapter to the subject of collecting Limoges. When Oprah recommended this book to her viewers, millions of her fans were exposed to Limoges. In 2001, Limoges Antiques Shop was featured in *The Wall Street Journal*, *TEA A MAGAZINE*, *Victorian Homes*, and in the best selling book, *Turn Your Passion Into Profits*. With this type of national exposure to the appropriate target market, any product would reach a newfound level of popularity. With an art form as beautiful as Limoges, the popularity has increased to new heights and the demand for certain pieces has exceeded the supply.

For today's Limoges collector, the reproduction problem is vast. Searching through common Internet auction sites, you will find most of the pieces to be reproductions and not nineteenth or twentieth century Limoges. All pieces are being reproduced, with the most popular being decorative pieces, vases, urns, tea and chocolate sets, punch bowls, trays, shoes, and boxes. Most of the pieces are decorated in cobalt blue, cranberry, and pinks surrounding a transferred scene or floral design, encased in gold. Among the most common fake marks are the fleur-de-lis, printed in gold and blue above a banner stating LIMOGES CHINA"; a mark with a crown above what could be interpreted as crossed swords over the word "LIMOGES" printed in gold; and the "ROC LIMOGES" or "ROC LIMOGES CHINA" mark. These marks are commonly over the glaze and you can feel them when you run your finger over the top. In contrast, the factories in France place their factory marks on the blank prior to firing, so the marks are under the glaze and cannot be felt. With reproductions flooding the Internet, such pieces have also begun to show up at most antique shops, flea markets, shows, and auctions.

One of the most common reproduction Limoges marks on the market today is the crown and crossed swords with the word "Limoges." For more on reproduction marks, see the section on "Common Reproduction Marks" at the end of the book.

Most collectors can tell a piece of authentic Limoges by the blank (the shape of the piece) or the quality of the decoration, but are reassured by the mark placed on the bottom. However, some of the early factories did not mark their pieces and some of the individual pieces in a set were not marked, so becoming familiar with common Limoges blanks and the differences between the look of reproductions and a true Limoges piece may prove helpful. Part III of this book, "Collecting Limoges," will help you in identifying Limoges blanks.

Antique Limoges pieces in cobalt blue, red, or cranberry have always been limited in production—they are the most expensive and very desired. These dark and dramatic colors have long been coveted and only the wealthy could afford a set with such elaborate coloring. The cobalt color was a very difficult color to achieve in the nineteenth century. Cobalt was applied under the glaze, and had to be fired at least twice. Many antique pieces have a shadow where the cobalt has run into the translucent porcelain. Also, if not stored properly over several decades, antique cobalt dinnerware will show wear from the pieces being rubbed against each other. In addition, darker colored dinnerware pieces may show knife cuts, making these pieces not as desirable. Reproduction pieces decorated in the cobalt blue or red color look perfect.

Antique pieces of Limoges, whether decorated by the transfer method or hand painted, had any gold gilt applied after the initial decoration. Pieces were embellished with lavish gold on the handles or trimmed around the edges, and some had raised gold paste scrolled to give a cameo appearance. Antique nineteenth and twentieth century Limoges pieces will look as beautiful as the day they were produced, unless they have been damaged. It is, however, very common to have some form of wear on the gold. For example, handles and rims of vases that have been lovingly used over the last hundred years may show signs of wear. Minimal gold wear that is obviously due to the use of a piece does not detract from the overall value. The lavish gold now has a rich patina look, in contrast to a reproduction, which will have a bright, offensive gold. Being aware of the differences between antique Limoges and reproductions can save a collector from purchasing unwanted pieces.

Today, the Limoges region of France is still considered the Mecca for hard paste porcelain and there are approximately forty working factories in the city of Limoges. Remember, when buying a new piece of Limoges at an exclusive boutique, Tiffany's, or a fine department store, you are purchasing a piece of fine hard paste porcelain produced in one of these factories. There is a huge difference between buying a new piece of Limoges and buying a reproduction, an inferior product not produced in France. The new Limoges dinnerware is dishwasher safe, making sets of Limoges desirable to a new generation. Boxes, table pieces, tea and coffee sets, and dinnerware are examples of pieces currently being produced. With improved technology and market exposure to a practical and beautiful art form, the twenty-first century may well be defined as "the golden era for Limoges."

Part II

Decorating With Limoges

The Entryway ~ An Invitation into the Living Room or Parlor

Whether located in an historic Victorian dwelling or new construction, the entryway is an invitation into a home and its living areas. The entryway can set the mood for a home: inviting, formal, intimate, casual, cluttered, or sparse. It is also a wonderful area for displaying a favorite collection or a single piece of Limoges. Colors can be used to evoke certain moods; using pieces with dark colors against a light wall, for example, makes the pieces really pop and a collection the focal point of the room. A monochromatic color scheme can make a room seem more serene and romantic. Use of the same colors or colors that complement each other will make the flow from an entryway into the living room or parlor seem coordinated and well thought out.

Large staircases are perfect areas for displaying pieces of Limoges art, such as chargers, plaques, and painting on porcelains. Landings are the perfect location for large pieces of Limoges—a jardinière or vase, perhaps—that will make a dramatic statement. Keep in mind that large staircases, large entryways, and large walls can handle larger pieces or even collections of Limoges placed in groupings. Smaller areas can be used for smaller collections housed in cases or vitrines that are proportioned to the space but large enough to hold a vast collection of tiny pieces of art on porcelain. A single piece of Limoges makes a statement, especially if the theme of the piece complements the other pieces of art, fabric, wall coverings and antiques in the room. A cherub hand painted on a plate is the perfect complement for a room or staircase where cherubs are the overall theme.

Fireplace mantels in any room are wonderful places for displaying collections. Large pieces evoke a mood of stateliness, a pair of vases provides balance, and a small collection can be combined and nestled amongst the larger pieces—especially if the mantel is large enough to handle several collections. Crystal and porcelain are a perfect combination. Grouped together, paintings on porcelain, paintings on canvas, porcelain miniatures, and miniature paintings on ivory create a unique and personal mantel.

The color schemes in the wall covering, rugs, window treatments, and pieces of upholstered furniture should be complementary to each other and to the collection you are displaying. A similar theme makes for a more formal living room. Creating sitting areas in cozy corners that include personal collections or a prized piece makes for a very interesting and unique room. Placing large pieces of porcelain on top of cabinets, under pieces of furniture, or on the floor makes the entire room a virtual display cabinet. Relying on a few helpful principles—such as using odd numbers of pieces together and varying heights and shapes—will help you compose lovely vignettes of Limoges in any room.

Entrance into the carriage house of The Castle, currently a private residence. The carriage house was built in 1906, using steel and concrete, allowing for the weight of six touring cars. The door was brought down from the castle upon its razing in 1941, and has been welcoming people into the carriage house, now a magnificent home, ever since. A beautiful entryway cabinet is perfect for housing a collection of Limoges, along with cranberry and ruby glass.

Rare majolica light fixtures, of museum quality, complement this lovely Limoges vase and cake plate. Both pieces of Limoges are artist signed by French factory artists and are investment quality.

The living room is a showcase for a Limoges collection, with numerous pieces nestled amongst a collection of paintings on ivory. An immense working fireplace of mahogany woodwork and Italian marble is the focal point. This fireplace was dismantled from the original castle and then lovingly placed, pieced by piece, into the carriage house. A fabulous pair of matching Limoges vases, with factory artist signatures, provide the appropriate formal statement on this magnificent fireplace mantel.

An original Currier and Ives painting proudly hangs above a miniature collection that includes a lovely hand painted Limoges portrait brooch and paintings on ivory of women from a similar era. The painting above the antique chest balances the verticality of the fireplace wall. An antique pink satin glass lamp provides romantic lighting for the corner and highlights this lovely collection of miniatures.

A chair upholstered in a light fabric lightens the dark room and provides dramatic contrast to the dark mahogany carved woodwork, antique oriental area rug, and wall treatment. A large Limoges vase of importance is a must on this fantastic mantel. Limoges boxes and brooches share space with miniature paintings on ivory on the side tables and tabletops.

Framed miniatures of elegant European ladies hand painted on ivory and porcelain are grouped together in random order. All four of the portraits are of young woman from an era long gone.

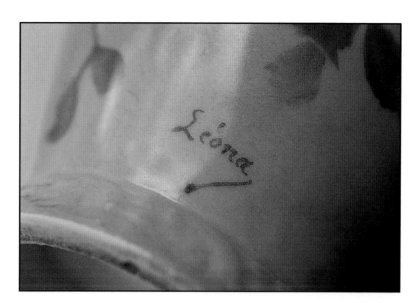

Factory artist signature "Leona" written in script on the side of the 14" tall Limoges vase. Most factory artists signed their pieces in black script on the front of the piece.

Below:
Limoges cake plate, 12" from handle to handle, factory hand painted. Underglaze factory mark in green, "PM DE M" with "Limoges France," P.M. Mavaleix Mark, ca. 1908-1914. Overglaze factory decorating mark in green, "Limoges" over the Coronet crown with "France," George Borgfeldt, Coronet Mark 1, ca. 1906-1920. $350-$550.

Left:
Limoges vase, 14" tall, J.P.L. France, Jean Pouyat Mark 5, ca. 1891-1932, "Hand painted" written in script on bottom and factory artist signed "Leona." $650-$950.

Beautiful living area with warm, rich, dark mahogany woodwork and dark red wallpaper provides dramatic contrast to an off white couch. Dark accent pieces such as pillows and cranberry Limoges boxes show the attention to detail of this collector.

Quality antique glass pieces, including vases, biscuit jar, oil lamp, and a Limoges jardinière holding a house plant, give this room a unique feel that the owners, dedicated collectors, welcome.

A large Tiffany leaded glass window becomes the focal point for this sitting area. Paintings on porcelain and ivory are unique pieces of art that keep the grouping from being perfectly square. A portrait plate continues the portrait theme from above and a large Limoges punch bowl on the floor gives this room a personal touch with character.

A cranberry glass lamp stands behind a grouping of miniatures, including three antique Limoges boxes. Cherished collections of porcelain and paintings on ivory and glass are placed throughout, evidence that this room is an intimate gathering spot.

Nineteenth century Limoges box in the shape of a heart, with portrait of a couple courting. Desirable and rare heart shape, undetermined markings, ca. nineteenth century. $400-$600.

Egg shaped Limoges box, purchased in Limoges France in 1973. Inscribed "Joyous Noel" and French factory artist signed. Underglaze factory mark in green, Limoges France, Mark 1, ca. after 1891. Overglaze "Porcelaine de'core'e la a' main Paris Style." $300-$400.

In 1941, these exquisitely detailed nineteenth century Tiffany leaded glass windows, originally in The Castle, were dismantled and incorporated into the carriage house renovations of the 1940s, which included this fabulous sitting area.

Beautiful Tiffany stained glass windows have birds, peacocks, baskets, and flowers in their design. The dramatic colors in the windows make a perfect backdrop for this mammoth Limoges vase with peacock decoration, hand painted by an amateur American artist.

The antique Persian carpet complements the cranberry and gold fabric of the drapes and the coordinating window seat covers. Rich gold tassels and trim on the window treatments match the stripes in the fabric below and are perfectly coordinated with the gold fabric in the chair. Warm rich colors make this elegant sitting area an inviting showcase that most would hire a professional decorator to achieve.

Mammoth Limoges vase, 18" tall, hand painted with a majestic peacock in opalescent shades of pink to various shades of purples. Marked D&C, Délinières Mark 3, ca. 1894-1900. Vase is on a base of matching pink opalescent color. This type of base was normally used under a jardinière. $1,500-$2,500.

Grand entrance into a Victorian Queen Ann home. This collector has decorated her fireplace mantel and entryway with Limoges pieces all decorated by the same artist. The vases, plaques, and other pieces are all factory decorated and signed by the French listed artist Ted Alfred Bronssillon, 1859-1922.

The large size of this formal Victorian style living room enables the owner to arrange two distinct sitting areas. A pair of cranberry chairs near the piano complement the ornately carved cherry parlor set with original green mohair upholstery. Plump pillows and stool with the settee, along with antique needlepoint pillows on the matching chairs, add color and texture to the front sitting area. The antique carpet placed on the floor provides the necessary warmth needed to make a room of this size more intimate. Dark pieces of Limoges add drama and pop out against the white walls.

Left:
A grand foyer sets the tone for a formal living room in this newly constructed Victorian style home. A beautiful Limoges hand painted punch bowl sits on a marble top, pedestal type table with two matching needlepoint chairs on either side acting as bookends. A hand made Portuguese rug called the "Seminario" adds warmth to this large area covered by a marble floor.

A pair of matching green chairs have needlepoint pillows perched on their arms. The colors complement the hand painted roses on the large Limoges planter on base sitting on a nineteenth century Victorian marble top table. A Limoges "muscle" vase is perched on the mantel shelf. The fabulous collection of Limoges along with art on the walls add a personal touch, making the room less sterile as well as creating a dramatic statement on the stark white walls. This is an original oil painting called "The Corner" by Susan Rios.

Left:
Large Limoges pieces look stunning on this fireplace mantel. Pieces that are unique in shape or size, perhaps with ornate handles and similar color tones, can hold their own when near original pieces of art on canvas. Chairs placed on either side of the fireplace enhance the focal point of the room: for the decorator, the fireplace; for the collector, the large Limoges jardinière at its base.

Limoges vase, 8.5" tall, serpent shaped handles and hand painted roses. Underglaze factory mark in green, J.P.L. France, Jean Pouyat Mark 5, ca. 1890-1932. $550-$750.

Limoges bowl, 14" diameter, has "T&H" embossed in the porcelain, ca. 1894-1957 with the overglaze factory decorating mark in red, Theodore Haviland above Limoges France, with "Pat applied for" ca. 1895-1903, artist signed "Leon." $495-$595.

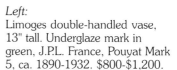

Left:
Limoges double-handled vase, 13" tall. Underglaze mark in green, J.P.L. France, Pouyat Mark 5, ca. 1890-1932. $800-$1,200.

Large Limoges 13" tall planter on original base, hand painted by an amateur artist. Underglaze mark in green, Limoges over W&G France, Guérin Mark 3, ca. 1900-1932. $2,000-$2,500.

Limoges ewer, 14.5" tall. Underglaze factory mark in green, W.G.&Co., France, William Guérin Mark 2, ca. 1891-1900. $700-$900.

Grand entry into this antique colonial home calls for massive pieces of Limoges that make a statement of formal elegance. A large Limoges vase placed on the floor has a mate perched on the landing high above.

Below:
A mix of contemporary and antique furniture creates a unique and individual style in this room. A formal sitting area nestled in front of the large bay window is "picture perfect." Coordinating pillows add color and texture to the off white walls, upholstery, and window treatments.

The off white upholstery contrasts wonderfully with the carved mahogany wood on the chairs. A mahogany table is placed between the two chairs and a dramatic Limoges plaque—factory hand painted with dark, vivid, life-like roses—sits on top.

French doors lead into the warm, rich, and light living room, where a needlepoint rug and pillows create a casual, yet elegant feel. A large gold framed mirror above the fireplace provides symmetry, a pair of huge Limoges vases act as sentinels on the mantel, and a large factory hand painted Limoges punch bowl is perfect to complement the room's color scheme.

The Limoges plaque, with thick gold border, is complemented by the gold vase and the gold handles on the Limoges bouillon cup with saucer, making a perfect vignette on this tabletop.

Limoges plaque, 10.5" diameter, factory artist signed A. Broussillon. Overglaze factory decorating mark in green, "Limoges" over the Coronet crown with "France," George Borgfeldt, Coronet Mark 1, ca. 1906-1920. $595-$695.

Above and right:
Limoges Vase, 22.5" tall, front and reverse.

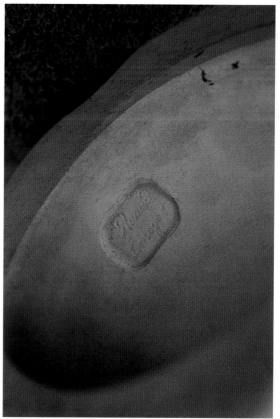

Left and far left:
Limoges Vase, 22.5" tall, front and reverse.

Unique mark is impressed into the porcelain in the base of each vase, illegible word above "Limoges."

Below:
Entry into this large Victorian home is breathtaking. Guests are greeted by a large mahogany staircase with double railings, carved banisters, and step treads of mahogany. Centered between the banister and frieze border, framed botanical prints are hung on the wall. Hung above the prints are three Limoges porcelain plates. The odd number and unique placement of the plates above the framed art make an interesting arrangement. Adding a bit of whimsy to what could have been an overly formal atmosphere, this collector perched her beloved rooster on the first step.

Right:
The large staircase calls for a gigantic piece of Limoges. At the top of the stairs, seen through the carved mahogany banister, is a massive gold Limoges jardinière on original base. This oversized jardinière, hand painted with gold gilt and cranberry flowers in a very distinct Art Deco style, fits perfectly on the ledge placed at the top of the landing.

Above right:
Gigantic Limoges jardinière on matching base with paw feet has elephant heads on both sides that act as ornate handles. Jardinière, 17.5" tall x 19" handle to handle. Underglaze factory mark in green, D&Co., Délinières & Co., Mark 1, ca. 1870s. $3,500-$4,500.

Right:
Lovely living area has a wealth of Limoges accessories, color coordinated with the couch and loveseat to unify the room. An antique mantel clock is centered on the fireplace mantel, with stately porcelain vases placed at either end. The lightweight window treatments provide lightness around the room with a floral fabric selected to relax the mood.

Right:
Below the gold framed mirror is a lovely antique lace covered table. This collector has placed a large jardinière between two hand painted American Belleek vases. The basic decorating principle of using an odd number of pieces makes a bold statement with lots of decorating impact.

Above left:
Fabulous Limoges lamp with new shade is a converted Limoges vase, 11" tall with double serpent handles. Underglaze factory mark in green, J.P.L. France, Pouyat Mark 5, ca. 1890-1932. $500-$900.

Left:
The large living area can handle a massive china cabinet placed against a wall. This antique, bow sided, quarter sawn oak china cabinet with applied carvings has five shelves that are perfect for displaying the vast collection of lovely hand painted Limoges. The large piece provides needed balance in the room and complements the large brick fireplace directly across from it. A notable feature of this room is the number of windows. An oval, gold framed mirror has been placed in between two of them, utilizing the space well.

Right:
Victorian oak china cabinet is used to display this homeowner's large collection of hand painted Limoges. It is one of the nicest collections of unique pieces owned by a private collector.

Three-handled loving cup, 6" tall. Underglaze mark in green, T&V Limoges France, Tressemann & Vogt Mark 7, ca. 1892-1907. $300-$350.

Ornate three-handled loving cup, or small vase, 7" tall. Underglaze mark in green, T&V Limoges France, Depose, Tressemann & Vogt Mark 8, ca. 1907-1919. $550-$750.

Ornate three-handled loving cup, or small vase, 7" tall. Underglaze mark in green, T&V Limoges France, Depose, Tressemann & Vogt Mark 8, ca. 1907-1919. $550-$750.

Right:
Victorian elegance, along with a large collection of Limoges, ensure this Victorian lover's look of charm and utter clutter. Large Limoges portrait vases stand on a nineteenth century hand painted tabletop and smaller pieces are safe inside a French vitrine.

A living room ready for the holidays. The fireplace mantel has been marbleized to match the marble columns standing at both sides. Both columns proudly display large jardinières on bases, while the fireplace mantel holds rare and unique pieces of Limoges that complement the raspberry colors in the room. Adorned with fringed shawls and lamp shades, this living room is reminiscent of days gone by.

Beautiful hand painted cookies from the Yummy Mummy Cookie Factory in Andover, Massachusetts look like tiny wrapped treasures sitting on top of the Limoges gold and cranberry cookie plate. Tea is ready to be served out of an ornate, all gold teapot. On the chair, antique postcards bearing holiday greetings are held in a rare Limoges letter holder.

In unusual holiday spirit, this collector has used her beloved Limoges teacup collection as ornaments on the tree. Each cup is hand painted and is as individual as the artist who created it. Mingled among the Limoges are hand blown glass birds of all varieties perched on the branches. Carved glass roses are used as lights, making a unique and beautiful holiday tree.

Hot chocolate is ready to be poured from this beautiful, ornate Limoges chocolate pot with matching teapot (not shown), sugar and creamer. All of the pieces are sitting on a large ornate Limoges tray with gold handles. Complete set $2,500-$3,500.

Limoges portrait vase, 13" tall.
Underglaze factory mark in green,
J.P.L. France, Pouyat Mark 5,
ca. 1890-1932. $1,000-$1,400.

A French vitrine is the perfect shape and size for
placement in the corner of this lovely entryway.
Safely out of the way of family and friends, an
exquisite collection of smaller porcelain pieces is
placed on the vitrine's shelves. A large Limoges
jardinière sits on the floor.

Beautifully polished hardwood floors create a formal living area. The
nineteenth century gold gilt French cabinets, hand painted desk and rare
music cabinet have been carefully selected to display this collector's
beloved collection of hand painted Limoges. A large painting on porcelain
hangs above a Limoges ewer and pitcher on a beautiful Limoges tray. A
massive Limoges jardinière on base sits on the floor below.

An archway leads directly into the dining room. The Limoges collection in the living
room is the perfect complement to a feast for the eyes in the adjoining dining room.

A French nineteenth century gold étagère has beautiful pieces of Limoges placed on the shelves, and a grouping of Limoges chargers hangs on the wall above. An unusual nineteenth century gold gilt cabinet houses a small collection of Limoges.

The fabric on this pair of tufted continental chairs from the 1930s is the perfect blue to coordinate with a Limoges vase placed between them. A Victorian shawl with long fringe adds romance to this sitting area.

Inside the unique gold cabinet is this wonderful group of Limoges pin trays, bowls, mirrors, covered jars, and boxes. Prices range from $25-$250.

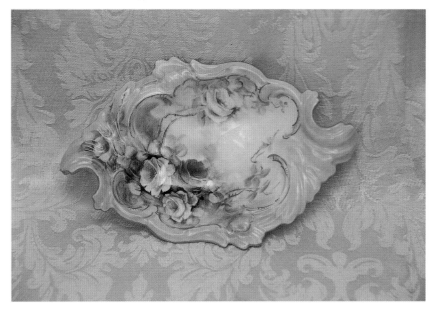

Limoges nut bowl, 2" x 3". Underglaze factory mark in green, T&V Limoges France, Tressemann & Vogt, Mark 7, ca. 1892-1907, amateur artist signed J.A. Barbour. $195-$225.

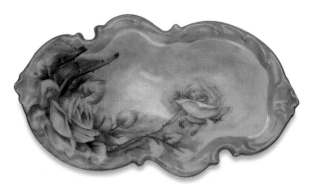

Small oblong Limoges bowl, 1.5" x 3" underglaze mark, D&C France, Mark 3, ca. 1894-1900 with illegible amateur artist initials. $75-$195.

Marks found on the bottom of the vase. Underglaze mark in green, Limoges Castel mark, ca. 1955-1979, and the words "Décor Main" (hand painted), literally meaning decorated by hand.

Limoges jardinière, 8" tall. Underglaze factory mark in green, France, Klingenberg, Mark 5, ca. 1890s, amateur artist signed "Corlus '09.'" $1,200-$1,500.

Limoges hand painted vase, 12" tall. Factory deco-rated, underglaze mark in green, Décor Main Limoges France, the Limoges Castel mark, ca. 1955-1979 and after, signed on front "F. Poujol." This is an example of a piece of Limoges that would be considered "new," in contrast to an antique piece from the nineteenth or early twentieth centuries. $350-$650.

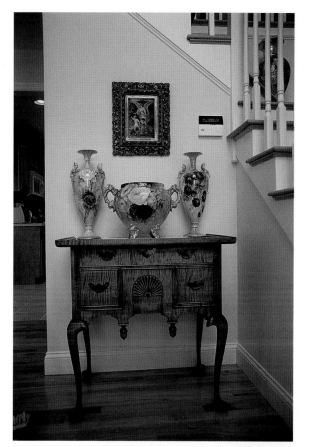

This magnificent entryway with staircase is located in a newly constructed modern home and can easily display large pieces of porcelain. Elegance abounds with a Waterford chandelier, custom made pieces of furniture, and a serious collection of Limoges porcelain. A slate top, tiger maple lowboy greets guests with three large pieces of porcelain.

Large Limoges jardinière on base, 8" x 12". Underglaze factory mark in green, D&C, Mark 1, ca. 1870s, amateur artist signed "Chamberlein." Jardinière with base and matching tray: $3,000-$3,500.

A pair of American Belleek vases proudly stand on either side of this ornate Limoges jardinière. Jardinière, 11" tall, D&C., Délinières & Co., Mark 3, ca. 1894-1900. $2,500-$3,500.

Tiger maple spoon foot tea table perfectly displays a large Limoges planter, 14" tall, W.G.&Co., Limoges France, William Guérin Mark 3, ca. 1900-1932. $1,500-$2,000.

The same tea table can also display a Limoges jardinière, 8" tall x 12" diameter, with gold lion head handles. Underglaze factory mark in green, D&Co., Délinières & Co., Mark 1, ca. 1870s. $3,500-$4,500.

Limoges jardinière, 8" tall x 10" diameter, with elephant head handles, proudly displaying gorgeous yellow roses. Underglaze factory mark in green, D&Co., Délinières & Co., Mark 1, ca. 1870s. $2,000-$3,000.

Modern living room, with custom furniture and an antique oak china cabinet placed between two of the many windows in the room, is perfect for displaying this colorful Limoges collection.

The top of the china cabinet is perfect for displaying large pieces of hand painted Limoges: a punch bowl and two vases of matching blanks, hand painted by two different amateur artists. Beautifully painted punch bowl on unusual base: $3,500-$4,500.

The oak china cabinet is full of beautiful hand painted Limoges porcelain. A lovely punch bowl on base, with matching cups, is on the bottom shelf. Bowl with matching cups: $2,500-$3,000.

Another view of this lovely living room with French doors.

In the center of the room, a large round tiger maple table acts as both coffee table and display table for a large Limoges double-handled vase. The vase is 18" tall, Elite L France, Bawo & Dotter Mark 5, ca. 1900 and Elite Limoges France mark in red, Bawo & Dotter, Mark 8, ca. 1896-1900. $2,000-$2,500.

Reverse of the vase.

Another beautiful tiger maple table serves as the perfect stage for this large, 17" tall Limoges vase. Beautifully hand painted, the vase is a perfect example of an unmarked Limoges blank. Soft colors are repeated in the pillow placed in the overstuffed chair—simple elegance.

A collection of unique pieces of Limoges are grouped on a covered table in the corner, safely tucked between two couches. A cup and saucer, two dessert plates, a tankard, ewer, and large Limoges vase make up this lovely vignette. Prices range from $50 for the cup and saucer to $2,500 for a punch bowl of this size with beautiful hand painted roses.

From a whimsical entryway to a fun living room. Balance is achieved by the picture placement on either side of the fireplace. Placement of a small vase and plate, both with cherubs, continue the theme from the entryway into the living room.

Incorporating hand painted furniture with large pieces of Limoges creates a feeling of whimsical elegance in this entryway to a newly constructed Victorian style home.

Lovely hand painted Limoges vase is complemented by the Limoges lamp attributed to amateur artist E. Miler. A pair of Limoges paintings look perfect hanging on the wall between the window treatments comprised of off white lace panels.

Antique Grandmother's clock is hand painted with roses, women, and cherubs. The theme is continued with the placement of a Limoges hand painted cake plate, also with a woman and cherub, on the wall nearby.

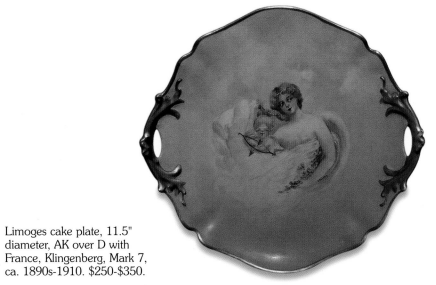

Limoges cake plate, 11.5"
diameter, AK over D with
France, Klingenberg, Mark 7,
ca. 1890s-1910. $250-$350.

This large modern entryway with
staircase can house large pieces
of furniture and large pieces of
Limoges. A mammoth chandelier
and original pieces of art are the
focal points of the staircase. A
very large 18" Limoges plaque
draws the eye to the entry wall.

Limoges vase, 16.25" tall, Limoges
France with W.G.&Co., Guérin, Mark
3, ca. 1900-1032. $700-$1,400.

Mammoth Limoges plaque, 18" diameter. Underglaze factory mark in green,
Flambeau China, Mark 3, ca. 1890s to
early 1900s, hand painted and signed by
factory artist Dubois. $2,500-$3,500.

A fireplace mantel in this large living room acts as the perfect perch for a collection of Japanese and Nippon moriage. Large Limoges plaques, chargers, and plates are hung on the walls, providing balance to the large, gold framed mirror above the fireplace. A Limoges punch bowl sits on top of a rare Korean lacquered chest used as a coffee table.

Another view of this elegant living room, with double doors leading into the library. Bronze statues are integrated into this porcelain collector's home.

Unusual Limoges punch bowl on base, 16" x 9.5". Underglaze mark in green, T&V Limoges, Tressemann & Vogt Mark 4, ca. 1892-1907. Raised enamel paint on the outside and unique whimsical painting inside. Amateur artist signed L. Vance Phillips, and dated 1906. $2,000-$3,000.

Large casual living area is ideal for decorative pieces of Limoges and makes hosting an afternoon Victorian tea seem easy and fun.

Beautiful set of six hand painted Limoges teacups, saucers, and dessert plates are set out on a low contemporary table. This hostess uses her finest: a sterling silver tea set and Limoges serving pieces. Sterling is a wonderful complement to fine hard paste Limoges porcelain and these antique pieces make for a most elegant afternoon tea.

Limoges punch bowl filled with fruit is perfect next to the fireplace. The fruit in the bowl matches the fruit hand painted on the outside of the bowl. $1,500-$2,000.

Lovely corner china cabinet serves as a display case for these two large Limoges punch bowls with matching tray and cups. $3,500-$4,500 each set.

Hand painted dessert set for six includes cups, saucers, and matching dessert plates. Underglaze mark in green, T&V, Tressemann & Vogt Mark 7, ca. 1892-1907. $700-$1,400.

Entry into this home looks directly into the living area. A lovely mahogany antique table holds a lamp created from a Limoges tankard.

Light wall coverings and a monochromatic color scheme help provide a feeling of openness as this contemporary living room flows directly into a lovely dining room.

Limoges tankard converted into a lamp, 16" tall, J.P.L. Limoges Mark 3, ca. 1896-1890. $495-$795.

Two other chairs are placed against the opposite wall; an antique sewing table with Limoges inserts sits between them. On the sewing table is a 6" Limoges vase marked D&C France. Pairs of chairs placed on opposite sides of the room help create a sense of balance, though not an exact mirror image. Completing this area is a very rare Limoges wall hanging. Round, 22" piece of Limoges in 28" gold frame. Artist signed "T.Leroy," very rare detailing of pate-sur-pate. $4,500-$6,500.

Guests to this home are greeted by a Limoges charger flanked by a reverse painted Pairpoint puffy lamp and Pairpoint glass handkerchief box that complement the colors in the stained glass window behind. The details of the collection on the table might be overlooked if the table were more ornate. The window molding is painted to match the color in the adjoining living area. Large charger, 18" diameter with roses, underglaze factory mark in green, T&V Limoges France, Mark 7, ca. 1892-1907. $600-$800.

Lovely gold gilt vitrine is flanked by two Victorian needlepoint chairs on either side. Placing the chairs directly under the windows provides symmetry and gives this room a balanced look. The rare Limoges piece on the wall becomes the center of attention when placed directly above the grouping on top of the cabinet.

Rare, 13" vase hand painted with four Arabs, two camels, and a Nubian slave woman. Pairpoint Limoges mark, ca. 1880s. $2,500-$3,000.

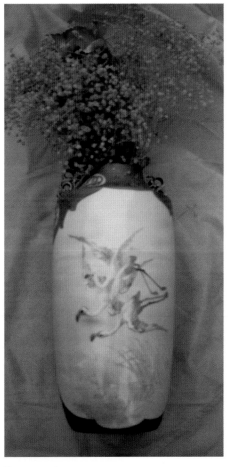

Reverse of vase.

Limoges pate-sur-pate of nymph and cherubs, white on cobalt, unframed dimensions 9.5" x 12"; in new frame, 16" x 18". Piece purchased in Limoges France directly from the factory. $295-$395.

The Dining Room ~ Limoges on the Tabletop

The dining room is not only the natural setting for Limoges dinnerware, it is the perfect room to adorn with decorative pieces of complementary Limoges art. Sideboards, china and display cabinets, vitrines, and tea carts can neatly hold large collections without the feeling of clutter. Large pieces displayed on top of such furniture give a dramatic look to a large dining room. Small display cases made specifically for collections of miniatures fit perfectly into a more modest sized dining room.

Grouping pieces with similar colors together will give your dining room display a more formal look. Mixing various colors of like items together makes for a more casual and fun look. Making sure the colors complement the room's overall theme will help you achieve a complete look that decorators are often hired to attain. Limoges plates or paintings on porcelain hung in a vertical line can create a unique ribbon effect between narrow windows. Groupings of Limoges using odd numbers of pieces, varying heights and shapes all with similar decorations, or items painted by the same artist are signs of a longtime collector with good decorating style.

The focal point of this room is definitely the set dining room table. Table art is another way of expressing oneself artistically and showing off a collection of Limoges. Setting the table with hand painted Limoges dinnerware mixed with crystal bowls and stemware evokes a formal dining atmosphere. A matching punch bowl in the center of the table makes a breathtaking statement. Tiny hand painted salts, butter dishes, and individual salt and pepper shakers make dining fun yet intimate—no detail is overlooked. Limoges dinner plates made for the American market are larger than Limoges dinner plates not made for export. A larger dinner plate with a thick rim of gold makes a dramatic statement when used as a charger under a completely different set of Limoges dinnerware. A vase with fresh flowers placed in the center of the dining room table exemplifies the beauty of Limoges art. And all dining rooms look fantastic with a well proportioned punch bowl or jardinière sitting dramatically alone on top of the dining room table, lit up by the light fixture above. Whatever your lifestyle, using your dinning room as another room to display a collection makes this room as unique and individual as you are.

An intimate sophisticated dining room, with an air of elegance and formality, is the perfect setting for this cranberry Limoges dinnerware set. Dark wall coverings are accented by moldings painted in a champagne color and window treatments with matching fabric, lined with cranberry.

A built-in china cabinet houses a collection of cranberry glass. The red of the glass complements the red crystal in the chandelier above, the lusters on the sideboard, the Limoges dinnerware, and the plates framed on the wall. The antique carpet under the table softens any hard lines of the room.

Fabulous, rare Limoges ewer, 15" tall, with hand painted portrait of a nude woman encased in raised gold paste, enamels of unusual green and raspberry. Reverse side of the ewer has hand painted roses cascading down an urn. Overglaze factory mark in heavy gold, Limoges above a crown with CORONET, France, ca. 1906-1920. $2,000-$2,500.

Another view of the dining room. Portraits of family members long passed hang on the wall to watch over intimate family dinners.

Lovely tabletop is set for formal dining. The Limoges dinnerware set coordinates with the colors in the room and looks perfect when mixed with antique pieces of cranberry glass and sterling flatware. Decorative pieces of Limoges mingle with a vast collection of miniature paintings on ivory. Between the windows is a rare miniature case with original cranberry velvet lining.

Rare, large Limoges palace urn, 20" tall and 11" from double gold handle to handle. Hand painted in exquisite detail and artist signed on the front "Guillou," reverse side has scene that includes a castle in the background. Underglaze mark in green, T&V Limoges, Tressemann & Vogt Mark 4b, ca. 1892-1907. $5,000-$9,000.

A gigantic Limoges punch bowl is an ideal centerpiece for this table set for the holidays. One end of the table is set with a Limoges hot chocolate service for eight, including chocolate pot, cups, saucers, and dessert plates.

Large colorful Victorian dining room is perfect for entertaining. Carved mahogany benches are substituted for traditional dining room chairs and a hand made needlepoint rug is used as a table covering. Large rooms can handle massive individual pieces as well as large collections of Limoges, especially when housed in, and on the top of, china cabinets.

Sideboard is placed in a bay window, making use of sometimes wasted space. On top is a dramatic vase and a beautiful collection of Limoges mixed with a pair of Waterford candelabras and sterling silver tea service.

Beautiful set of cranberry or red Limoges dinnerware for eight includes 11" dinner plate, 8" salad or dessert plate, and 6" bread and butter plate. Factory mark in red, Charles Field, Haviland, Limoges, Haviland Mark 3, ca. 1941. Set: $595-$795.

Limoges 8" salad or dessert plate from set.

Limoges 11" dinner plate from set.

Limoges dessert set for eight includes 8" plate, 6" plate, cup and saucer, and matching teapot with sugar and creamer. Underglaze factory mark in green, Bernardaud & Co., Mark 1, ca. 1900-1914. Set: $1,500-$2,000.

Fabulous Limoges 12" cranberry dinner plate with raised gold paste and hand painted center medallion of flowers. Limoges W.G.&Co., France, Guérin Mark 3, ca. after 1900-1932. Overglaze import mark, Martin's Detroit. Set of twelve: $2,200-$3,000.

Limoges 8" dessert plate from set.

Victorian dining room has a beautiful mantle decorated for the holidays with fresh greenery and yellow roses. More yellow roses are on the table, along with wedding band Limoges cups and saucers that have been in this Rowley, Massachusetts family for four generations.

Beautiful 12" dinner plates have transferred gold etching in a 1" border, with lifelike hand painted roses in the center. Set of twelve: $1,200-$2,400.

The table's unique centerpiece includes a functional Limoges gravy boat nestled on top of the greenery and yellow roses. The hand painted roses on the dinner plates emulate the real roses in the centerpiece.

This dining room in a dark, dramatic Victorian home with tin ceiling features a large antique oak dining room table and matching pressed back chairs, sideboard, and china cabinet. In the center of the table is a fabulous hand painted Limoges punch bowl with roses. Custom made drapes with fabric complementing the colors in the antique oriental carpet beneath the table add to the drama of the room.

Three distinct Limoges tankards. Each is unique, marked with a factory under and overglaze mark, and factory artist decorated and signed. $1,500-$1,900 each.

Antique oak sideboard with applied carving is perfect for a Limoges tankard collection, ewer, and planter all with similar colors of red, cranberry, and pink hand painted roses.

The focal point of this dining area is a large ornate sideboard with dramatic Limoges cider pitcher and matching mugs—the perfect complement to the Bradbury and Bradbury hand designed wallpaper. Set: $1,295-$1,500.

On the dining room table is a mammoth Limoges jardinière with lions' head handles on a matching base with large gold paws. The decorator selected this particular piece to match the heads on the dining room chairs.

Formal dining takes place in this elegant dining room with off white moiré taffeta drapes featuring champagne fringe that matches the wall covering. A needlepoint rug provides a more relaxed look to the room and is placed under the antique table and chairs, a family heirloom shipped here from Europe. A Limoges jardinière on the table adds art and color to the monochromatic room.

Another view of the Limoges jardinière with lions' head handles. Underglaze factory mark in green, D&C Mark 3, ca. 1894-1900. $2,500-$3,500.

Limoges jardinière, 11" tall, on base with paw feet. Underglaze factory mark, D&C France, Délinières & Co., Mark 3, ca. 1894-1900. $3,500-$4,500.

Beautiful Limoges 8" factory hand painted scalloped plate sits on top of a 10.5" Limoges dinner plate, one from a set of ten. (A 12" dinner plate was selected to be used as a charger.) The dinner plate and matching cup and saucer have the Ahrenfeldt Mark 8b. Set: $1,800-$2,000.

Hand painted 9.5" Limoges plate. Underglaze Haviland factory mark and artist signed. $295-$395.

An upholstered window seat with contrasting fabric pillows makes a cozy, yet light and airy sitting area. The artwork is made up of two dramatic hand painted and artist signed Limoges pieces that introduce new color to the room.

Limoges 9" scalloped plates with hand painted scenes of a man and woman in the middle of the plate, surrounded by a scrolled cameo of raised gold gilt. Set of twelve, each unique, with underglaze factory mark in green, Elite L. France, Mark 5, ca. after 1900, and overglaze factory decorating Mark 9 in red, ca 1900-1914. Each hand painted and signed on the front by factory artist "Patllet." This is a great example of a Limoges plate that was decorated in the factory, hand painted and artist signed. $195-$225 each.

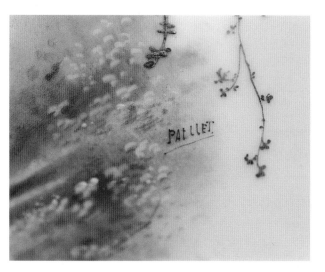

Factory artist signature on the front of the portrait plates.

Shown are both the factory and decorating mark on the back of the plates: underglaze factory mark in green, Elite L. France, Mark 5, ca. after 1900, and overglaze factory decorating Elite Works Limoges France Mark 9 in red, ca 1900-1914.

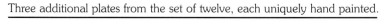

Three additional plates from the set of twelve, each uniquely hand painted.

Classic stripes add whimsy and charm to this elegant home with an eating area in the family room. Decorative Limoges pieces with red and white roses match the strong colors in the stripes, but provide some softness and curvaceous lines. An antique oriental rug adds warmth to this large size room.

Limoges chocolate pot with four of the eight cups and saucers in the set. Underglaze factory mark T&V Limoges France, Tressemann & Vogt Mark 7, ca. 1892-1907. Overglaze factory mark with banner stating "Hand Painted" Tressemann & Vogt Mark 16b, ca. 1907-1919. Set: $2,000-$3,000.

Beautiful decorative pieces of Limoges—tankard, chargers, ice cream platter, and chocolate pot with cups and saucers—are placed on the table. All of these pieces have the Tressemann & Vogt factory mark under the glaze, T&V Limoges France Mark 7, ca. 1892-1907, and the red Tressemann & Vogt factory mark over the glaze, with the banner "Hand Painted" Mark 16b, ca. 1907-1919. These pieces date to 1907 and have various factory artist signatures from the Tressemann & Vogt factory. Prices run from $495 for chargers to $2,000 for a complete chocolate set.

A solid color couch between two windows, flanked by a pair of floral love seats, creates a cozy sitting area of perfect symmetry in this large room. A very rare pair of Limoges tables are placed directly in front of the couch. The current owner purchased them from a man who had inherited them in 2001 from his mother's estate. The heir remembered these tables being purchased in a Boston antique shop in the 1950s.

One of a very rare pair of Limoges tables, 22" tall, top is bolted to base, both pieces are marked Limoges France, Castel Factory Mark ca. 1955-1979. The top and the base are hand painted with flowers with ornate gold scrolling. Factory decorated, unique, and very desirable. $1,000-$2,000 each.

Mark on the base of the table, Limoges France, Castel Factory Mark, ca. 1955-1979.

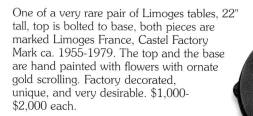

Mahogany sideboard displays a punch bowl on base, vase, and Bradley and Hubbard leaded glass lamp—a lovely invitation into the dining room.

Mark on the underside of the tabletop, Limoges France, Castel Factory Mark, ca. 1955-1979.

Ornate Victorian oak sideboard on one side of the center window provides balance and a wonderful home for Limoges collections ranging from a hot chocolate set to chargers and plaques.

Victorian dining room is perfect for this large collection of Limoges. All of the room's moldings, doors, and window frames are original, beautifully polished hardwood with carved medallions. A highly polished hardwood floor is home for a beautiful antique oriental rug with antique oak dining room table and chairs centered over the rug's center medallion. The table is lit by a beautiful brass antique chandelier with original glass globes. Wallpaper is an original Bradbury and Bradbury design with the owner's family crest proudly displayed within the ceiling's design.

Lovely tabletop set with all marked Theodore Haviland Limoges dinnerware. The set is "The Belfort" pattern marked with Mark 57 incised and Mark 34, ca. 1904-mid 1920s. This set includes dinner plates, salad or dessert plates, bread and butter plates, soup and salad bowls, double-handled bouillon cups with saucers, cups and saucers of various sizes, chocolate pot, teapot, cream and sugar, covered dishes, various sizes of platters, gravy boat, and butter pats. Complete set with 225 pieces, service for twenty. $1,000-$2,000.

Balance is achieved by using two massive pieces of nineteenth century oak furniture on either side of the window. The china cabinet with top and five shelves can hold various groupings and large amounts of Limoges porcelain while acting as a bookend to the oak sideboard.

Large Limoges hand painted jardinière, 9" tall. Underglaze factory mark in green, D&Co., France Délinières & Co., Mark 3, ca. 1894-1900. $1,000-$1,500.

A small antique table is flanked by two pressed back oak dining room chairs, making a charming grouping for this wall space between a window and door. On the wall is a large watercolor in a gold frame with thick gold mat. Two Limoges paintings on porcelain fill the space on either side of the painting and a large 18" round plaque is placed above, continuing the romantic theme. This busy wall needs no competition, so a single piece of decorative Limoges, a large 10" jardinière, is placed on the table below.

This collector loves pieces from the Jean Pouyat factory. Shelf is filled with a fourteen-piece ice cream set consisting of twelve white and gold transferred filigree 8.5" plates, matching platter, and sauce boat. Underglaze mark J.P.L., Pouyat Mark 5, ca. 1891-1932, overglaze mark J.P.L., Pouyat Mark 9, ca. 1914-1932. Set: $300-$600.

Various pieces of like decoration from the Jean Pouyat factory sit on this shelf. Set of six 8.75" dessert plates have transfer pink roses with transferred gold embellishment and hand painted gold trim on the edges. Underglaze J.P.L., Pouyat Mark 5, ca. 1891-1932, overglazed J.P.L., Pouyat Mark 9, ca. 1914-1932. Single plate, 9.75" with transfer pattern, underglaze mark, J.P.L., Pouyat Mark 5, ca. 1891-1932 and overglazed J.P.L., Pouyat Mark 9, ca. 1914-1932. Large 12" serving bowl, underglaze mark J.P.L., Pouyat Mark 5, ca. 1891-1932, overglaze mark J.P.L., Pouyat Mark 9, ca. 1914-1932. Individual transfer decorated Limoges pieces from dinnerware sets continue to be a great buy—making a set table beautiful and unique. $25-$100 each.

Set of four 9.5" luncheon plates with hand painted roses and teal background. Underglaze mark J.P.L., Pouyat Mark 5, ca. 1891-1932. $75-$100 each.

Set of six 9.75" luncheon plates with transfer decoration of small roses and dark green background. Underglaze factory mark in green, J.P.L., Pouyat Mark 5, ca. 1891-1932 and overglaze J.P.L., Pouyat Mark 9, ca. 1914-1932. $60-$100 each.

Dining room, situated off of the formal living area, uses a complementary color scheme allowing for the flow from one room to the next. One large Limoges punch bowl is all that's needed to provide a dramatic tabletop statement.

Amateur artist hand painted Limoges 12" tall punch bowl on base. Underglaze factory mark T&V Limoges, France, Tressemann & Vogt Mark 7, ca. 1892-1907. $2,500-$3,000.

Sideboard with mirror centered above reflects a beautiful hand painted Limoges vase and lamp. This collector favors Limoges pieces that are hand painted and signed by amateur artist E. Miler.

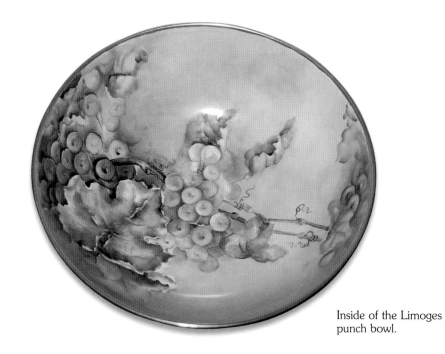

Inside of the Limoges punch bowl.

Limoges bowl on feet, artist signed "E.Miler." Underglaze factory mark in green, J.P.L., Pouyat Mark 5, ca. 1891-1932. $125-$200.

Close-up of amateur artist E.Miler's signature.

Fabulous contemporary dining room is done in off white tones; wooden slat window blinds are dressed up with sheer lace panels that allow light in through the windows. A large oak pedestal table in the corner houses a mammoth porcelain vase that adds color and drama to the room. Against the wall, a custom made tiger maple table proudly displays a beautiful hand painted punch bowl on matching tray.

This round table and two Victorian chairs make a charming vignette, perfect for the magnificent punch bowl on base with matching cups.

The dining room table is set with individual style and beauty, using E.Miler pieces painstakingly acquired by this devoted collector. Waterford crystal bowls and stemware are the perfect complement to the Limoges dinnerware. A beautiful oil painting in an ornate gold frame is centered on the all white wall. Simply elegant is the statement this room makes.

Beautiful Limoges punch bowl and place settings of hand painted porcelain, artist signed by E.Miler.

Unusually large Limoges punch bowl, 16" diameter and 7" tall, on matching tray. Underglaze factory mark in green, W.G.&Co., Guérin Mark 2, ca. 1891-1900. Set: $2,200-$3,000.

Closer view of 9.5" Limoges plate, artist signed by E.Miler. Table set with matching teapot, creamer, sugar, cup and saucer, bread and butter plates, and other service pieces all artist signed by E.Miler. Complete set for six: $2,500-$3,500.

Custom drop leaf table made of tiger maple is a piece of art; add the magnificent punch bowl on stand, tray, matching cups, lamp, and vase and you create a breathtaking opulence.

In the background, a beautiful hand painted punch bowl, 6.5" x 13", artist signed by Yvonne Klapec. Underglaze factory mark in green, T&V Limoges France, Depose, Tressemann & Vogt Mark 8, ca. 1907-1919. $3,500-$4,500. Overglaze decorating mark, Tressemann & Vogt Mark 16, ca. 1907-1919. In the foreground, a rare Limoges domed cheese dish with cover, 5.5" tall, artist signed "E.Miler." Underglaze factory mark in green, P P LA SEYNIE, ca. 1903-1917. $395-$595.

Close-up of the hand painted Limoges punch bowl on stand (shown above right), 8.5" x 13", underglaze factory mark in green, T&V Limoges France, Tressemann & Vogt Mark 7, ca. 1892-1907. Set includes 3.25" high cups, Bavarian mark, and a large, 17" diameter tray. The tray is marked with the underglaze factory mark in green, GDA, Gérard, Dufraisseix, and Abbot Mark 1, ca. 1900-1941. This is an example of an amateur artist who selected blanks from different factories and hand painted them as a set. Set: $4,500-$5,500.

Limoges jardinière on base, 11" x 12". Underglaze factory mark in green, D&Co., France, Délinières & Co., Mark 3, ca. 1894-1900. $2,500-$3,500.

Formal dining area has archway into the living room; colors were chosen to blend with both areas. The dining room table is exquisitely set with hand painted pieces of Limoges, all beautifully painted by amateur artist E. Blanche McFeely. All pieces have the Limoges factory underglaze mark but, since they were not decorated in the factory, none have the overglaze decorating mark.

Huge Limoges jardinière is the centerpiece for this lovely tabletop. Elaborate crystal candelabras on both ends of the table and unique crystal glasses make an elegant tabletop.

Limoges covered tureen, 7" x 9". Underglaze factory mark in green, T&V, Tressemann & Vogt Mark 8, ca. 1907-1919, signed "E. Blanche McFeely." $695-$795.

Unusual Limoges bowl, 3.5" x 9", painted inside and out. Underglaze factory mark in green, T&V, Tressemann & Vogt Mark 8, ca. 1907-1919, signed "E. Blanche McFeely." $495-$695.

Limoges cracker jar, 6.5" x 9" from handle to handle. Underglaze factory mark in green, T&V, Tressemann & Vogt Mark 8, ca. 1907-1919, signed "E. Blanche McFeely." $495-$695.

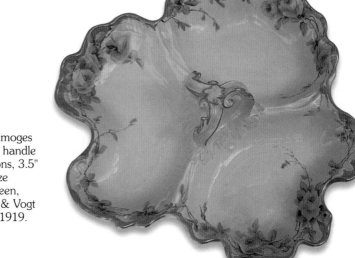

Unusually large Limoges serving piece with handle and divided sections, 3.5" x 14.5". Underglaze factory mark in green, T&V, Tressemann & Vogt Mark 8, ca. 1907-1919. $795-$995.

Limoges pudding bowl, 5.5" x 9", ornately painted inside and out. Underglaze factory mark in green, T&V, Tressemann & Vogt Mark 8, ca. 1907-1919, signed "E. Blanche McFeely." $495-$695.

Tressemann & Vogt underglaze factory Mark 8 in green, ca. 1907-1919 and sample of amateur artist E. Blanche McFeely's signature.

Fabulous large dining room is the perfect place for formal dining. Moiré walls between the dental molding and chair rail emphasize the height of the room. The table is centered directly below a massive chandelier and a breakfront is placed on the far wall, perfect for this homeowner's large collection of Limoges.

Lovely tabletop set with Limoges hand painted porcelain dinnerware: dinner, salad, and bread and butter plates, soup bowls, cups and saucers, salt and pepper shakers.

Dark green tablecloth adds softness to the room while providing a dramatic background for the hand painted Limoges dinnerware. A large porcelain turkey is the perfect centerpiece for this Thanksgiving table. It is flanked by two tall American Belleek vases on either side.

The hand painted Limoges dinnerware makes this table look like a work of art. Set of ten 12" Haviland factory marked dinner plates, hand painted with roses, are artist signed "Sargeant" and dated 1907. Set: $1,500-$2,000.

Unique hand painted serving bowl, 8.5" x 12.5", complements the dinnerware set. It is amateur artist signed and marked Elite France. $495-$695.

Beautiful hand painted bowl on feet makes a perfect serving piece. Hand painted cup and saucer is part of a complete set for six with the GDA factory underglaze mark. Set: $1,200-$2,000.

Fabulous eighteenth century mahogany game table is used to display these wonderful Limoges plaques, 16" diameter, artist signed "Dubois." $3,500-$4,500 each.

Limoges basket, 8.5" tall. Underglaze factory mark in green, J.P.L., Pouyat Mark 5, ca. 1891-1932. $395-$495.

Limoges nappy, 7.5", factory decorated. Underglaze mark in green, J.P.L., Pouyat Mark 5, ca. 1891-1932. $75-$125.

Limoges covered jar, 6.5" x 9" from handle to handle. Underglaze factory mark in green, T&V, Tressemann & Vogt Mark 8, ca. 1907-1919. $495-$695.

Limoges basket, amateur artist painted. Underglaze factory mark in green, star with Limoges France, Coiffe Mark 3, ca. after 1891-1914. Price according to the quality of hand painting: $195-$495.

Beautiful hand painted Limoges vase is the eye-catching centerpiece for this table set with Limoges dinnerware decorated in the factory using a transfer ware pattern. Mixing decorative pieces of hand painted Limoges with factory decorated dinnerware makes for a practical and beautifully set dining room table.

A monochromatic color scheme was used in this small, smartly decorated dining area. The owner brightened the room by covering the walls in a light, softly colored wallpaper. The tiny pattern in the wallpaper coordinates with the floral pattern in the Limoges dinnerware set. This factory decorated dinnerware set has been passed down through three generations. Set: $595-$795.

The factory decorated dinnerware set has a matching teapot, sugar and creamer, and cups and saucers. These pieces would have been purchased separately to match the dinnerware set. Today, sets such as these can be found from $295-$495.

Complete transfer ware dinnerware set. Underglaze mark in green, Elite/L/ France, Bawo & Dotter Mark 5, ca. after 1900. Overglaze decorating mark, Bawo & Dotter Mark 9, ca. 1900-1914. Set: $595-$795.

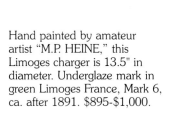

Hand painted by amateur artist "M.P. HEINE," this Limoges charger is 13.5" in diameter. Underglaze mark in green Limoges France, Mark 6, ca. after 1891. $895-$1,000.

Hand painted Limoges vase, 14.5" tall. Underglaze factory mark in green, PL, Limoges France, La Porcelaine Limousine Mark 1, ca. 1905-late 1930s. The amateur artist left his or her initials, "NDSG," hidden among the flowers. $1,000-$1,500.

Rare Haviland Limoges cobalt cup and saucer. Underglaze mark CFH/GDM Haviland Mark and overglaze factory decorating mark in blue, CH FILED HAVILAND, LIMOGES, ca., 1859-1881. $295-$395.

Elegant Victorian home's dining room has carved moldings and ceiling medallions, plus window treatment on the large bay window that matches the chair seat covers. Centered between two windows is a serigraph by Marc Chagall, titled *Tribe of Gad*. An elegant oriental rug beneath the table grounds the entire room.

The tabletop is set with rare antique cobalt Limoges dinnerware—money was of no consequence for the original owners of these magnificent and rare plates. Raised gold enamel detail on the cobalt dinner plate is highlighted by mixing bread and butter, salad, and dessert plates with heavy gold trim. With no detail overlooked, rare cobalt serving pieces, a very rare Theodore Haviland cup and saucer with raised gold and white enameling, crisp linen, crystal, and the family sterling complete this elegant table.

Set of rare bouillon cups and saucers, each hand painted with a beautiful woman in the center of a cameo of raised gold paste with enameled dots and a garland of flowers flowing around the cup and saucer. The original set consisted of twelve, each hand painted with a different portrait. Underglaze factory mark in green, Haviland France, ca. 1910-1924. $295-$395 each.

Lovely gold coffee pot marked "Limoges" is surrounded by a set of cobalt demitasse cups, lined with gold, and their matching saucers. Pot $195-$295.

Set of twelve demitasse cups and saucers in their original presentation case. $1,500-$2,000.

Two additional cups and saucers from the set.

Close-up of demitasse cup and saucer. Underglaze mark Limoges France with double SS, Siegel & Sohm Mark, ca. 1906-1923.

Limoges dessert or salad plate, 7.5" with thin cobalt trim. Underglaze mark in green, Vignaud Frères, Mark 3, ca 1938, overglaze Wanamaker's import mark in green. Set of ten: $125-$350.

A trio of antique Limoges dinnerware pieces. The cobalt blue color is very desirable, collectible, rare, and valuable. This color is, however, found on many reproductions. It is important to familiarize yourself with the blanks, marks, and characteristics of antique cobalt pieces, such as the blue color running into white translucent areas.

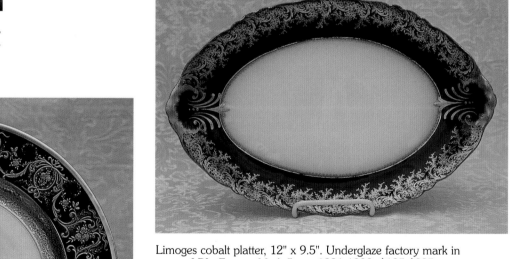

Limoges cobalt platter, 12" x 9.5". Underglaze factory mark in green, J.P.L. France, Mark 5, ca. 1891-1932. $195-$295.

Limoges 12" cobalt dinner plate with thick raised gold paste (back side of the plates have a gold rim). Underglaze mark in green, Ahrenfeldt Mark 6, ca. 1894-1930s, overglaze decorating Mark 8a, ca. 1894-1930s. Set of twelve: $2,000-$2,500.

Limoges 11" cobalt dinner plate. Underglaze factory mark in green, Limoges, WG&Co., France, Guérin Mark 3, ca. after 1900-1932. Overglaze decorating mark in red, Guérin Mark 4, ca. 1800s-1932. Set of twelve: $1,200-$1,500.

One from a set of six, 11" Limoges dinner plates. Scalloped edge with cobalt rim, underglaze factory mark in green, Haviland &Co., overglaze factory mark in red, Haviland & Co., ca. 1888-1896. Set of six: $695.

Limoges 11" cobalt dinner plate with center gold medallion. Underglaze Ahrenfeldt, Mark 5 in green, ca. 1894-1930s, overglaze Boston import mark. Set of twelve: $1,500-$2,000.

Left:
One from a set of six, 11" Limoges dinner plates. Underglaze factory mark in green, H&Co.,/L. Haviland & Co., Mark 9, ca. about 1878. Overglaze decorating mark in red, Haviland & Co., Limoges, Haviland & Co., Mark 13, ca. 1876-1930. Set dates to about 1878. Set of six (color and marks affect value): $1,295-$1,795.

Right:
Limoges tray, 8" x 10". Underglaze Pairpoint mark, ca. 1880s. $595-$695.

The Kitchen

Today, the kitchen seems to have become the family room—the room where everyone congregates. Decorating this room can be as fun as decorating any other room of a house, and bringing Limoges into the kitchen provides style, inspiration, and personality. Carrying the overall color scheme into this room is nice but not a must if the kitchen is a separate room, unseen from other areas. Placing china cabinets, desks, tables, and other pieces of furniture in the kitchen ensures that there is room to display a collection. In new construction, built-in cabinets with rails that can house punch bowls, trays or a teapot collection are a must. The Victorian home provides the perfect kitchen for antique china cabinets or a working antique stove; such pieces can supplement missing countertops and add cabinet space.

If your kitchen has a fireplace, decorate the mantel with unique pieces of Limoges art in groupings. A plate, vase, and tray can form an interesting grouping with different shapes but similar colors that also coordinate with the room's overall color scheme. Varying sizes of Limoges art create interesting and unique groupings. Plates, plaques, chargers, and paintings on porcelain are perfect wall decorations. Using pieces of Limoges as borders above archways, windows, mantels, and sinks makes the kitchen a beautiful, as well as useful, room for family and friends to congregate in.

Charming kitchen with a large bay window allows for a poolside view. The large jardinière was selected to coordinate with the window treatment and makes a dramatic statement as the focal point on the table. Throughout the kitchen, Limoges plates and chargers are integrated with other pieces of blue and white porcelains.

This large eating area has sliding glass doors that look out over the beautiful and well manicured grounds. In winter, this spectacular antique china cabinet, chock full of Limoges, replaces the outdoor view.

The collector uses every inch of space in this large antique oak sideboard.

The china cabinet is placed at an angle, allowing a view of the living/family room and formal dining area. The softly muted floral wallpaper was selected not to compete with, but to enhance the beauty of the flowers in the Limoges.

The wall covering was chosen by this serious collector to enhance the beauty of the Limoges punch bowl and charger.

Limoges biscuit jar complete with lid, 7.25" tall. Underglaze factory mark in green, T&V Limoges Mark 7, ca. 1892-1907. $295-$395.

Another hand painted covered vegetable bowl or dish, 9" x 5.25". Underglaze Haviland & Co., Mark I, ca. 1894-1931. $295-$595.

Dinnerware pieces from a set include this beautiful hand painted covered vegetable bowl or dish, 9" x 5.25". Underglaze Haviland & Co., Mark I, ca. 1894-1931. $295-$595.

Limoges 12" cake plate, beautifully hand painted and artist signed "G. Lykes." Underglaze factory mark in green, Paroutaud, Mark 2, ca. 1903-1917. $225-$295.

Casual kitchen breakfast area is set with beautiful pieces of Limoges, including a large decorative jardinière, 11" tall, with ornate handles. Underglaze factory mark in green, D&Co., Délinières & Co., Mark 3, ca. 1894-1900. $2,500-$3,500.

The kitchen island displays beautiful decorative pieces of Limoges: a vase with hand painting of a woman and cherub that matches the scene on a large 11" jardinière. Underglaze factory mark in green, D&Co., Délinières & Co., Mark 3, ca. 1894-1900. $2,500-$3,500.

Large 14" Limoges tray is used to hold a crystal decanter and glasses, ready for serving in this lovely kitchen sitting area. $495-$695.

The island is fantastic for displaying a punch bowl, vase, and other pieces of beautiful porcelain.

A view of the island from the opposite side of the room, showing the reverse of the Limoges punch bowl and vase.

A feast for the eyes, the tabletop pieces includes a tankard, charger, vase, small punch bowl and hand painted berry bowl set. Prices range from $295 to $2,500.

Lovely eat-in kitchen area. Placed symmetrically at the windows are two similar marble top brass tables, each holding a large jardinière. The table is centered directly below the handcrafted chandelier. An elegant tablecloth makes this eating area romantic and inviting.

Individual Limoges place setting acts as "tabletop art" while waiting to be useful.

The kitchen table is now set for a casual yet elegant breakfast. A large Limoges punch bowl with under tray and matching vase are all hand painted with beautiful roses. Three large decorative pieces of this quality are very desirable.

Beautiful Limoges 9.5" J.P.L. dessert or breakfast plate is coordinated with an odd hand painted cup and saucer. $50-$75.

Closer view of the phenomenal punch bowl on stand with matching tray and vase. All pieces are hand painted by the same amateur artist. Pieces of this size and quality are very collectible. Punch bowl set: $3,500-$5,500. Vase: $1,500-$2,500.

This lovely hand painted jardinière was selected to coordinate with the wallpaper; the chair fabric was chosen to match Nicolas's beautiful blue eyes!

Beautiful Limoges cup and saucer, 2.5" tall. Hand painted inside and out, underglaze factory mark in green, J.P.L. Pouyat Mark 5, ca. 1891-1932. $75-$95.

Above right:
Fabulous eat-in kitchen has a wonderful leaded glass chandelier, attributed to Tiffany. This collector makes a dramatic statement by placing three hand painted Limoges punch bowls in the center of her round antique oak table.

Right:
Limoges punch bowls come in a variety of shapes and sizes; some blanks have a base, some have feet. These three bowls are each hand painted as uniquely as the artists' imaginations, with grapes of different colors and variations. Punch bowl prices range from $695-$3,500 and up.

This Victorian home's music room leads into the kitchen.

An antique stove in this kitchen is the resting place for this tray with lemonade for three. A beautiful floral arrangement from the owner's garden is nestled in a 5.5" tall Limoges mug marked J.P.L. and artist signed "L M N." Individual mugs from tankard sets range from $75-$195. Berry set consists of the master bowl and six berry bowls, factory decorated with Lily of the Valley, underglaze mark Mavaleix, P.M., ca. 1908-1914, overglaze Coronte Mark 1, ca. 1906-1920. Set: $295-$395.

Picture perfect, these goodies are not only on Limoges serving pieces, they are showcased by the light from a Limoges lamp.

Right:
A welcomed break becomes even more enjoyable with a Limoges mug bearing a hand painted Dutch scene with children, signed on bottom "Ethel M. Seeback," with T&V Mark 7c, ca. 1892-1907. Individual mugs from tankard sets $75-$195. An 8" x 8" Limoges planter with underliner continues the Dutch theme with a hand painted landscape of windmills. Underglaze mark J.P.L. Mark 5, ca. 1891-1932, signed "DC Tatlow 1910." $795-$1,500.

Eat-in kitchen provides a great area for displaying this collector's vast collection of hand painted Limoges dinnerware.

A different view of the table.

Complete dinnerware set of hand painted Limoges, a perfect example of an amateur artist who painted the entire set using many different Limoges blanks: D&C Mark 3, ca. 1894-1900, on the cups and saucers, gravy boat, covered vegetable bowl, and platters; Haviland Mark on the butter plate; Elite France, Bawo & Dotter, Mark 9, ca. 1900-1914, on the 8" plates and 12" dinner plates; J.P.L. Mark 5, ca. 1891-1932, on the 6" bowls. Set: $1,200-$2,000.

Beautiful 12" Limoges pitcher, underglaze mark in green H&C, Haviland Mark C, ca. 1876-1879 is hand painted in exquisite detail and sits on the window sill with a lovely cup and saucer. Pitcher $595-$795.

The Bedroom or Boudoir

The bedroom is a wonderful place for displaying a personal collection of Limoges. The privacy and romance of the bedroom can reflect a collector's love for particular pieces. Make the master suite an inviting and romantic retreat using coverlets, throws, and bedspreads with floral themes. Match the colors to a Limoges collection and the occupants will feel like they are sleeping in a garden. Dark dramatic spreads or stark white coverlets create inviting opulence and are perfect for enhancing a collection of Limoges. Large bedrooms are ideal for creating cozy sitting areas with tables, cushions, or stools, all perfect for displaying a Limoges punch bowl, chocolate set, or tea set. Imagine the collector's delight when, on a cold winter's eve, hot tea is served from a beloved teapot.

When present, a tall pillar, column, or pedestal in the bedroom can emphasize a massive vase, creating an impressive statement. Wall space is abundant in some bedrooms, perfect for showcasing an entire collection of chargers, plaques, or paintings on porcelain. These pieces of Limoges art make unique wall décor on painted or papered walls. Cozier rooms look lovely with a dresser set or diminutive pieces of Limoges art. Brooch and button collections placed on trays in the bedroom are art to the eyes. Side tables are just right for small collections, highlighted by a Limoges lamp. While matching pairs of lamps are very rare, decorating with lamps similar in color or theme creates dramatic—or romantic—lighting. Romance in the bedroom is inevitable when beautiful pieces of Limoges, from an era gone by, surround you.

Large bedroom suite is the perfect romantic retreat with a custom, hand carved, king sized bed as the focal point. Dark accent pillows match the window treatments and antique oriental carpets. Decorated with exquisite attention to detail, flowers in the ornate garland were color coordinated with the hand blown glass detail in the chandelier.

The sitting area is fit for a queen; the elegant chandelier above looks like her crown. Light colored moiré wallpaper ensures that elegance is the statement made by this room. Large pieces of Limoges are used as artistic accent pieces on side tables and on the tops of dressers.

The intimate feel of the sitting area is enhanced by placing an oriental run in front of the large window and centering a small loveseat between a pair of needlepoint chairs. The large Limoges punch bowl was chosen to match the color in the fabric of the loveseat.

Matching pair of hand painted Limoges lamps, 14" tall, with new custom made shade.

Limoges charger, 12.5" diameter. Overglaze factory mark, AK France, Mark 7, ca. 1890s-1910. $495-$695.

No space in this large room has been overlooked: the long Limoges painting on porcelain is perfect in this small corner, while the dresser top has an exquisite collection of porcelain that includes a Limoges charger with a scene that coordinates with the scene in the mirror above.

Right:
A closer view of one of the Limoges lamps, 14" tall. $495-$795.

Limoges painting on porcelain, 7" x 14" in original frame. Underglaze factory mark in green, J.P.L., Pouyat Mark 5, ca. 1891-1932. $1,200-$1,500.

Small groupings placed on walls between doors and closets personalize what might otherwise be an overwhelmingly large room.

This beautiful grouping of Rose Tapestry and tiny Venetian mirrors is the perfect place to integrate a tiny framed Limoges painting on porcelain.

Limoges painting on porcelain measures 3" x 6" unframed. Underglaze mark in green, T&V, Tressemann & Vogt Mark 7, ca. 1892-1907. $450-$600.

Heavy gold on the Limoges charger's rim is a perfect complement to the grouping of ornate gold caskets, mirrors, and perfume bottles from the 1920s and 1930s.

French hand painted table is lovely placed against this small wall. The large framed portrait of roses combined with a Limoges charger hand painted with roses makes a perfect wall grouping.

Limoges charger, 13" diameter. Underglaze mark in green W.G.&Co., Guérin Mark 2, ca. 1891-1900. Although unsigned, this is a beautiful example of a hand painted piece of Limoges painted by an unknown amateur artist. $800-$1,200.

The hand crafted poster bed in this large bedroom is elegantly covered in off white. A rare, 24" diameter painting on porcelain is centered above the headboard and two beautiful paintings on porcelain are appropriately placed on either side.

Custom bird's eye maple piece with mirror is placed between two doors. Richly colored porcelain items make a dramatic statement against the off white walls.

Sitting area in this lovely bedroom is perfect for enjoying a cup of hot chocolate from the Limoges chocolate pot placed on the nineteenth century marble top table. The rug was chosen to complement colors in the other pieces of hand painted porcelain in the room, including a beautiful Limoges punch bowl and cups.

Beautiful antique table looks perfect placed against this large wall. A grouping of three large trays is hung above the table with colors that complement the two Limoges vases and the Limoges planter below.

Pair of vases, 16.25" tall with the Guérin Mark 3, ca. 1900-1932, and hand painted by different amateur artists, act as bookends to a 12" tall Limoges planter. Underglaze factory mark in green, W.G. &Co., Guérin Mark 3, ca. 1900-1932. Vases: $1,500-$1,900 each. Planter: $1,000-$1,500.

A single Limoges vase with ornate double handles looks picture perfect in a corner of this room. Unmarked blank attributed to the Limoges factories. $1,000-$1,500.

Beautiful bedroom in a contemporary home is furnished with hand crafted bird's eye maple furniture mixed with antique pieces: a rocker, desk, and plant stand. Large decorative pieces of Limoges porcelain are displayed on the dresser and desk top.

On the floor of this collector's bedroom sits a large Limoges cache pot, 13" tall. Underglaze mark in green, W.G. &Co., Guérin Mark 3, ca. 1900-1932. $775-$995.

Hand crafted bird's eye maple bed with hand carved pineapples is a superb piece of art as well as the focal point of this bedroom. Accent pieces of Limoges are displayed in groupings on the individual hand crafted side tables and a Limoges lamp adds perfect lighting for the room.

A Limoges chocolate set, with 11.75" tall pot and matching cups, is displayed on this beautiful table. The set is factory decorated using the transfer ware method and has underglaze and overglaze factory marks from the Gérard, Dufraisseix, Abbot Factory. Set: $1,400-$1,500.

Fabulous bedroom in a large Victorian home uses gold as an accent color in the chair fabric and the curtains. The Limoges dresser set and tray on the wall also incorporate various shades of yellow and gold.

A rare three drawer French cabinet is used as a side table in the bedroom. Each of the drawer pulls has an insert of Limoges porcelain, individually hand painted with cherubs. A piece of furniture in this condition is highly sought after by collectors and has a value of $5,500-$6,500.

Left side of the cabinet.

Left and below:
Close-ups showing two of the
hand painted Limoges inserts.

Right side of the cabinet.

In this lovely bedroom retreat designed for that special teenager, a young collector displays her collection on the wall and bedside table.

This bedroom has a fabulous deco bedroom vanity with three-sided mirror, perfect for reflecting the three pieces of Limoges placed in a grouping.

Unique three-sided Limoges bowl is placed on a stand and is wonderful as part of a grouping that also includes a darling single Limoges demitasse cup and a heart shaped box on a Limoges tray. Individual pieces: $75-$325 each.

Maximum impact is achieved with the grouping of three vases in unique shapes and sizes, all hand painted in the same shade of peach.

Limoges vase, 9" tall. Underglaze factory mark in green, J.P.L. France, Jean Pouyat Mark 5, ca. 1890-1932. $600-$700.

Reverse of cachepot.

Limoges vase, 15" tall. Underglaze mark in green, W.G.&Co., Guérin Mark 3, ca. 1900-1932. $1,000-$1,500.

Limoges cachepot, 9" tall. Underglaze factory mark in green, W.G.&Co., France, William Guérin Mark 3, ca. 1900-1932. $600-$800.

An ornate hand painted Limoges tray has beautiful detail of exquisite raised gold paste. $225-$325.

This collector has coordinated her bedroom with window treatments in shades of peach to match the colors in the Limoges pieces sitting on an antique desk carefully placed between the windows.

Limoges jardinière in a unique small size, 9" tall on base. Underglaze factory mark in green, France, and base T&V Mark 7, ca. 1892-1907. $1,500-$2,000.

This antique porcelain doll watches over the Limoges dresser set.

Lovely guest bedroom has coordinated wall and window treatments that were custom made to match the bed covers. A Limoges dresser tray with hair receiver and covered jar sits on the bed waiting for the guest to arrive.

Limoges dresser set includes a tray with matching hair receiver and covered jar. Underglaze factory mark in green, T&V Limoges France, Tressemann & Vogt Mark 7, ca. 1892-1907. Three piece set: $395-$595.

Limoges dresser set includes 11" tray marked T&V Limoges France, hair receiver, small pin tray, and other covered jars all marked under the glaze P&P, Paroutaud Freres Mark 2, ca. 1903-1917, other pieces marked Bavaria. Complete dresser set: $395-$595.

Massive and ornate four poster cherry bed has two large antique tables on either side. Each table displays a grouping of Limoges, including a pair of hand painted Limoges lamps both artist signed "Michael."

A large Limoges punch bowl on tray, hand painted with roses, is carefully placed on the shelf under a large collection of smaller Limoges pieces. Punch bowl is 13" in diameter and has the T&V Limoges France, Tressemann & Vogt Mark 7, ca. 1892-1907. Tray is 14.5" in diameter, underglaze factory mark in green, D&Co., France, Mark 3, ca. 1894-1900. Set: $2,500-$3,500.

This romantic Victorian bedroom was featured in the 2001 Holiday Issue of *Victorian Homes*. A lovely Limoges dresser set sits on a Victorian, marble top table. Complete dresser set with candle holder and picture frame: $595-$795.

This sweet bedroom has a hand painted lingerie chest that coordinates perfectly with the bed covering. Above the bed is a hand painted portrait on porcelain. $2,000-$2,500.

Elegant breakfast tray for one; a Pairpoint Limoges cup and saucer serve as the focal point. $125-$175.

Dresser set includes a large 14" tray, hair receiver, two covered jars, and a pair of matching candlesticks, all factory marked under the glaze in green, T&V Limoges France, Tressemann & Vogt Mark7, ca. 1892-1907. Set with candlesticks: $795-$1,295.

A Limoges dresser set sits amongst a grouping of vases. Dresser set includes an 11" tray, pin tray, and two covered jars marked under the glaze D&C France, Mark 3, ca. 1894-1900. Set: $395-$595.

Fabulous collector's bedroom invites romantic dreams. The dark wall treatment is complemented by a floral bedcover and decorative pillows, giving this bedroom the look of a garden. A large painting is centered above the headboard, with Limoges plaques grouped on either side.

Two large Limoges plaques hung together look stunning on a side wall.

Wonderful Art Deco bedroom set includes this ornate dresser and mirror. The piece is perfect for displaying even more pieces of Limoges, which are beautifully reflected in the mirror.

Decorative Limoges lamp shines above a nice grouping of other Limoges pieces, including a charger, vase, and painting on porcelain. This collector attributes some of her decorating ideas to the tips she found in the book *Living With Limoges*, sitting on her tabletop.

Bedside table with hand painted Limoges lamp, plaque, and vase. The pieces range in price from $595-$995.

The Bath and Laundry Room

Limoges in a bath or laundry room is a great decorating choice. A collection displayed here is unexpected and can make these rooms as fun or as sophisticated as any other room in the home. Indeed, countertops become less conventional when a Limoges vase serves as the focal point. A Limoges collection displayed on the bathroom wall introduces personality in a room that is often overlooked. Romance is unexpected in the bathroom; add bubbles, candlelight, and a Limoges vase filled with romantic roses, however, and the unexpected becomes inevitable. Removing the doors from cabinets hung on the wall lets you display a beloved collection inside. Making the bathroom a showcase is not only fun, it allows a passionate collector to enjoy her collection while preparing for the day.

Laundry rooms are a necessity, and in some homes they are on the same floor as the living areas. Adding a Limoges collection to laundry room shelves or hanging pieces on the walls makes this room charming and a thankless task more welcomed—or at least adds the distraction of beauty. What a surprise to open the door and feast your eyes on a beloved collection or single piece of Limoges that beckons you into the room. Utility rooms are no longer just utilitarian when a piece of Limoges is displayed within them.

This collector has incorporated a collection of paintings on porcelain into the color scheme of the guest bathroom.

A Limoges hand painted tray with two matching brushes is perched on the bathtub ledge. Underglaze factory mark in green, T&V Limoges France, Tressemann & Vogt Mark 7, ca. 1892-1907. Set: $595-$795.

Left and above:
Limoges paintings on porcelain, 7" x 14"
in original frames. $795-$1,295 each.

Limoges 12" tray, kidney shaped, part of a set. Underglaze factory mark in green, T&V Limoges France, Tressemann & Vogt Mark 7, ca. 1892-1907. Set: $595-$795.

Above and right:
Limoges brushes, part of the set.

This large bathroom has an antique oak washstand with a Limoges vase, jardinière, and lamp displayed on top. A 14" tall Limoges cachepot is perfect for a collector's magazine rack. Pieces range from $795-$2,000.

In this true collector's bathroom, chargers with ornate borders and various size plates are used as art on the wall and above the mirror.

Fabulous hand painted vase is the focal point on the bathroom countertop.

Wonderfully elegant bathroom has a cathedral ceiling and large walls that provide the perfect canvas for a collection of uniquely shaped bowls, chargers, and plates.

Reflected in the large wall mirror, this unusual Limoges grouping doubles in impact.

Romance or just relaxation is imminent, with Limoges enjoyed by candlelight.

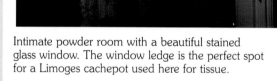

Rare Limoges three-sided bowl, 11" x 2.5", is marked with the underglaze factory mark in green, "Limoges France" Mark 3, ca. after 1891. The factory that decorated this piece placed their mark over the glaze in red "AK/CD Limoges France" Klingenberg and Dwenger Mark 9, ca. 1900-1910. The factory artist's signature is on the front of the piece. $495-$595.

Intimate powder room with a beautiful stained glass window. The window ledge is the perfect spot for a Limoges cachepot used here for tissue.

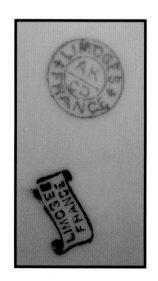

Factory marks on the bottom of the bowl.

Factory artist's signature on the front of the bowl.

This homeowner displays her collection of Limoges porcelain in the guest bathroom. Grouping pieces painted in similar colors and with the same type of flowers makes a major impact, particularly if the pieces are placed in an all white room.

Otherwise ordinary powder rooms become rooms worthy of a collection when fabulous Limoges pieces like this vase serve as focal points.

The daughter of this collector is overjoyed to include pieces of Limoges in her private bath. Limoges trays hold soap and other bathroom necessities, while a Limoges vase is reflected in the mirror.

To ensure that her guests feel welcome, this ingenious collector has transformed a Limoges planter into a tissue holder and a small vase into a brush holder. A tiny basket holds cotton swabs and wipes and a Limoges dresser tray with pin tray and hair receiver is perfect for holding rings and other sentimental pieces of jewelry.

This charming bathroom is in a vernacular Queen Anne home in Waltham, Massachusetts and was featured in the 2001 Holiday Issue of *Victorian Homes*. The lovely Limoges vase was selected to coordinate perfectly with the wall treatment.

Used as the master bath in the home today, the room retains an original corner cabinet. Perched on top is a lovely Limoges planter with swan handles, used exactly as it would have been in the nineteenth century—to hold a common house plant.

A hand painted piece of furniture is useful in the laundry room—
and also perfect for displaying this large 15" Limoges vase with the
Elite, Bawo & Dotter Mark 11, ca. 1920-1932. $1,200-$1,700.

Even the most practical areas of a home become enticing when Limoges
pieces are prominently displayed. This serious collector has a beautiful hand
painted ice cream tray with eleven plates displayed above his laundry room
cabinets and a fabulous Limoges vase placed between the washer and dryer.

Every corner is utilized when a serious collector is involved! Here,
a table of perfect proportions has been found and is now home to
a lovely Limoges vase and clock. Pieces: $595-$1,200.

This collector has paintings on porcelains displayed in her laundry room.

Pair of exquisite paintings on porcelain in their original frames. Pair: $1,500-$2,000.

The Porch or Patio

Collectors love to display Limoges in every room, using every inch of space—and that includes the porch or patio. The porch welcomes you home, the patio is the perfect retreat. Both of these places become even more inviting when romance and individuality are added by including a Limoges collection amongst flowers and furniture. Planters, jardinières, and ferners overflowing with seasonal flowering plants can be placed on the floor. Match the flowers to the decoration on your piece of Limoges and you have twice the beauty.

The patio is the perfect place for summer entertainment. A glass of lemonade served from a tray holding a Limoges tankard with matching mugs or fruit punch served in a large punch bowl make a hot summer day welcomed. An enclosed porch is an ideal winter retreat, a place to enjoy a steaming cup of hot chocolate served from a Limoges chocolate pot with matching cups and saucers. Using these rooms as extensions of the home creates unlimited possibilities for displaying a Limoges collection while making entertaining practical and easy.

Creating a room outdoors on a patio or porch is perfect for collectors; this area becomes an extension of the home and another area in which to display a beloved porcelain collection.

This beautiful table is set with hand painted Limoges dessert plates that match the tablecloth perfectly.

A Limoges vase or rose bowl makes a magnificent centerpiece. Underglaze factory mark in green, J.P.L. France, Pouyat Mark 5, ca. 1890-1932. $295-$495.

Large Limoges 18" hand painted tray was used to create a custom made table, perfect for holding a glass of ice tea or lemonade. $900-$1,000.

Nicholas, the family's beloved cat, is waiting for his "cuppa tea" to be served out of this lovely Pouyat Limoges teapot, artist initials "JRZ." $395-$595.

A 12" tall Limoges chocolate pot, with matching cups, saucers, and tray. All pieces have the underglaze factory mark in green, T&V Limoges France, Tressemann & Vogt Mark 7, ca. 1892-1907. Artist signed "Levy." Set: $1,000-$1,500.

A poolside party would be perfect in this screened in porch. A massive Limoges punch bowl, hand painted inside and out, was selected to coordinate with the fabric on the patio set.

Large Limoges punch bowl is marked under the glaze and is factory decorated; the artist's signature was on the punch cups, which have been separated from the bowl. Bowl without matching cups: $3,000-$3,500.

Patio dinning for two is romantic with Limoges dinnerware. This set was purchased because it is a perfect match for the fabric on the wicker chairs.

Beautiful 13" Limoges vase is perfect for holding tall flowers such as these gladiolas grown on the grounds of "Thousand Day Farm" in historic New England. $550-$750.

Hand painted with white and yellow chrysanthemums, this 8" x 11.5" Limoges jardinière is filled with real mums and greens right out of the collector's garden. Underglaze factory mark in green, J.P.L. France, Pouyat Mark 5, ca. 1891-1932. The lovely bowl is the focal point on the patio table and the perfect complement for artwork displayed on the nineteenth century music stand. $1,200-$2,000.

Left:
This Victorian home is on the National Register of Historic Homes and features a long wraparound porch in front—it's the perfect place for this home-owner to display her collection of Limoges planters and jardinières. $1,000-$2,000 each.

Below:
The porch is a great place to enjoy a glass of fresh squeezed lemonade. A Limoges berry bowl set holds fresh strawberries while a Limoges cake plate is used to serve cookies and a beautiful Limoges tankard acts as a vase. Individual pieces: $195-$395.

The owners of this center entrance Colonial home in historic Andover, Massachusetts make good use of the original porch, now screened in and updated for convenience.

Rare Limoges tankard set includes an 18" oval tray, 11.5" tankard, and six 4" matching mugs, all hand painted with water lilies and artist signed "SRS." Underglaze factory mark in green, J.P.L. France, Mark 5, ca. 1891-1932. Set: $2,500-$3,000.

A lovely Limoges punch bowl with base holds freshly cut garden flowers and is the focal point of the porch. $2,000-$2,500.

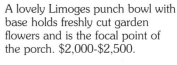

Uniquely shaped porch has been custom built on the front of this reproduction Victorian home. The collector searched the countryside to find unusual wicker pieces to furnish it.

Below:
To ensure that this collector can enjoy her "cuppa tea," even on days with inclement weather, an inside porch has been converted to a "tea room."

Part III
Collecting Limoges

Cake Plates

Cake plates normally run 10" to 13" in diameter, although a large 16" cake or serving plate is shown here. Most have some sort of serving handles and some of the most desired are on a pedestal. Cake plates were sometimes part of a complete dessert set, which may have consisted of the cake plate, cups and saucers, and dessert plates. A desired dessert set would also include the teapot, chocolate pot, or coffee pot, along with creamer and sugar.

Most factory dinnerware sets did not include the dessert set as part of the dinnerware set, but the dessert set was available to purchase separately. Many factory decorated cake plates and complete dessert sets are available to those antiquing today. A transfer ware cake plate can be purchased for under a hundred dollars, while a complete dessert set will run several hundred dollars. Factory hand painted cake plates run several hundred dollars, depending on the desirability of the artist and the quality of painting.

The amateur artist of the nineteenth and twentieth centuries could randomly select blank pieces of Limoges, thus creating her own distinct and unique dessert or dinnerware set. It was not unusual for an artist to have a hand painted dinnerware set that included a matching dessert set. Hand painted cake plates and dessert sets are very desirable. Not only do these lovely decorated pieces look fabulous hanging on walls, but when needed they can be called into usefulness. Individual hand painted cake plates run several hundred dollars with a complete dessert set running into the thousands, especially if a chocolate pot or teapot happens to be part of the set.

Example of a large 16" cake or serving plate. Artist's signature "March" on front. Underglaze factory mark in green, Depose Touraine T&V France, Tressemann & Vogt Mark 8.1, ca. 1892-1907. Unusual size is consideration when determining value: $750-$950.

Factory decorated cake plate, 12" diameter. Underglaze factory mark in green, Paroutaud Freres, Mark 2, overglaze Paroutaud decorating mark, factory artist signed on the front "Lafort," ca. 1903-1917. $275-$375.

Cake plate, 12" diameter, same blank as previous cake plate. Underglaze factory mark in green, Paroutaud Freres, Mark 2, ca. 1903-1917. This cake plate is hand painted by an amateur artist with unrecognizable initials on the back. $175-$275.

Cake plate, 14" diameter. Underglaze factory mark in green, J.P.L. France, Pouyat Mark 5, ca. 1891-1932. Amateur artist initials "EMB." $395-$495.

Cake plate, 11.5" diameter. Underglaze factory mark in green, T&V Limoges, Tressemann & Vogt, Mark 4, ca. 1892-1907. $195-$295.

Factory decorated cake plate, 13.5" diameter, Underglaze factory mark in green T&V Limoges France, Tressemann & Vogt Mark 7, ca. 1892-1907. Overglazed factory Mark 16 in purple ca. 1907-1919. Factory artist signed on the front. $375-$495.

Cake plate, 11.5" diameter. Underglaze factory mark in green, Haviland France, Mark I, ca. 1894-1931. $295-$395.

Chargers

Chargers, or chop plates, have become very desirable as pieces of art. Characteristically, chargers are a minimum of 12" in diameter and can be perfectly round or have scalloped or embellished edges. Prior to the Victorian era, chargers were specifically used as some form of platter, typically for meats. The factories that produced transfer ware dinnerware made matching chargers, chop plates, and platters that would match a set. Once the fad of china painting became popular in the United States, amateur artists began using this large round piece of porcelain as a canvas to hand paint and decorate.

Walls decorated with chargers can look unique and beautiful. Some chargers have been elegantly decorated with heavy gold gilt, creating a gold border. Others have been professionally framed, turning them into fabulous pieces of art. Using chargers to create a fantastic still life on top of a sideboard, cabinet, or vitrine can make a dramatic decorating statement. These diverse and unique pieces of art are as individual as the artists who painted them. Today, chargers range in price from several hundred to a thousand dollars and have become very popular as pieces of art to be hung on a wall, integrated into a collection, or displayed individually.

Charger, 14" diameter, hand painted by a professional factory artist. Underglaze factory mark in green, Tressemann & Vogt Mark 8, ca. 1907-1919. Overglaze decorating mark in red/purple, Tressemann & Vogt Mark 16, ca. 1907-1919. $600-$900.

Chop tray or charger, 13" diameter, hand painted by an amateur artist. Underglaze factory mark in green, J.P.L. France, Jean Pouyat Mark 5, ca. 1891-1932. $800-$1,000.

Charger, 14" diameter, hand painted by an amateur artist. Underglaze factory mark in green, AK over D with France, Klingenberg Mark 7, ca. 1890s-1910. $800-$1,000.

Left:
Charger, 14" diameter, hand painted by an amateur artist. Underglaze factory mark in green, AK France, Klingenberg Mark 7, ca. 1890s-1910. $800-$1,000.

Right:
Charger, 13" diameter, cherub hand painted by an amateur artist. Underglaze factory mark in green, T&V France, Tressemann & Vogt Mark 5b, ca. 1892-1907. Artist signature "Louise Tripler." $1,000-$1,500.

Charger, 16" diameter in frame, spider mums hand painted by an amateur artist. Underglaze factory mark in green, T&V France, Tressemann & Vogt Mark 5b, ca. 1892-1907. $1,000-$1,500.

Charger, 12.5" diameter, thick 4" gold border and flowers hand painted by an amateur artist. Underglaze factory mark in green, T&V France, Tressemann & Vogt Mark 5b, ca. 1892-1907. $800-$1,000.

Charger, 14" diameter in new custom 3" frame. Beautiful roses hand painted by an amateur artist. Underglaze factory mark in green, T&V France, Tressemann & Vogt Mark 5b, ca. 1892-1907. $1,500-$2,000.

Chalices

The pieces identified as chalices are normally 10" to 11" tall. All examples currently available in Limoges resource books are those hand painted by amateur artists. Some of these chalices are commemorative in nature, have a family crest or initials, and are hand painted very decoratively with fruit, berries, roses, or portraits. Amateur china painters painted pieces as uniquely as their imaginations. Most Victorians kept in mind the actual use of a piece, making the most essential utilitarian household item a decorative piece of art. The chalices painted with fruit and berries could have been used as some sort of drinking mug for an individual of wealth and prestige. The chalices painted with commemorative details and family information could have been used as a gift or simply a decorative piece to be placed on a mantel. Whatever the original intended use, today the chalice is a rare find and a beautifully decorated one can run $600 to $800.

Chalice, 10" tall, hand painted by an amateur artist. Artist's signature "S.N. Fanar." Underglaze factory mark in green, T&V Limoges France, Tressemann & Vogt Mark 7, ca. 1892-1907. $600-$800.

Chalice, 10" tall, dripping gold and enameled roses hand painted by an amateur artist. Underglaze factory mark in green, T&V Limoges France, Tressemann & Vogt Mark 7, ca. 1892-1907. $600-$800.

Chalice, 11" tall, hand painted by an amateur artist. Underglaze factory mark in green, T&V Limoges France, Tressemann & Vogt Mark 7, ca. 1892-1907. $495-$595.

Chalice, 10" tall. Hand painted by an amateur artist, grapes decorate this unmarked blank. $395-$495.

Chocolate Pots

During the Victorian era, it was customary for mothers to serve their children hot chocolate or cocoa as a breakfast or mid-morning beverage. In addition, the Victorians would sometimes serve hot chocolate as a substitute for tea during the afternoon. The French are credited with the design of a pot in the seventeenth century called a chocoliatiere. Today, this pot is commonly called a chocolate pot or cocoa pot.

When trying to determine if a pot is a chocolate pot versus a pot used for tea or coffee, simply look at the spout placement. The characteristics of the spout are consistent in most porcelain chocolate pots—it is close to the top of the pot and very stubby and short. Chocolate pots are usually tall and narrow and can range in height from 5.25" for a single pot, to 10" for a four cup pot, to 12" for a six to eight cup pot. The lid of the pot may have a factory placed hole for a long silver spoon to be inserted; the spoon was used to stir any chocolate that had settled on the bottom of the pot. Some pots do not have this hole—in this case, the spout was used for this purpose. Cups are distinctly taller than a teacup but hold a smaller amount and would match the decoration of the pot.

Factory decorated chocolate set includes 12" tall pot and eight 3.5" tall cups with saucers. Set also includes a matching 12" cake plate and five 8" and 6" diameter dessert plates. Underglaze factory mark in green, Coiffe Mark 3, after 1891-1914. Overglaze decorating mark in green, Flambeau China Mark 4, ca. 1890s-early 1900s. All pieces marked "Hand Painted" and are signed on the front by the factory artist "Henria." Set: $2,500-$3,500.

Hot chocolate was made during the Victorian era by roasting the cocoa shell, grinding it into a paste, then adding boiling water and maybe some milk or egg yokes, followed by confectioner's sugar. Sometimes the preferred method was melting shavings from a block of unsweetened chocolate in boiling water, then mixing in boiling milk and confectioner's sugar. The hot chocolate would be served on a tray and taken next to a fireplace. On the tray would be the cup on a saucer as well as a sugar and creamer, so that the level of sweetness could be adjusted to an individual's preference. Contrary to current popular belief, a complete chocolate set could include a sugar and creamer in addition to the pot, six to eight cups and saucers, and a tray.

A complete chocolate set today is very desirable, highly collectible, and expensive. A complete set can run several thousand dollars. Due to the high cost of a set, many sets have been broken up and the chocolate pot sold separately. A chocolate pot sold individually is priced from $295 to around $1,000. If it has matching cups, the price is increased based on how many matching cups accompany the pot. Price is based on uniqueness of the blank, condition, decoration, and whether cups, sugar and creamer, tray, or a dessert plate are included.

Chocolate set with pot and four matching cups and saucers, all hand painted with violets. Although this appears to be a Limoges blank, the pot is marked under the glaze with the Ginori mark.   Set: $1,000-$1,200.

Chocolate set with pot, six cups and saucers, and tray. Underglaze factory mark J.P.L. France, Mark 6, ca. 1891-1932. Set: $2,000-$3,000.

Unique chocolate pot, 11" tall, hand painted by
unknown amateur artist and unmarked. $295-$395.

Chocolate pot, 9" tall, hand painted by
unknown amateur artist. Underglaze factory
mark in green, Theodore Haviland, Limoges
France, Mark p, ca. 1903. $400-$600.

Chocolate pot, 9" tall. Underglaze factory mark in green,
D&Co, Délinières Mark 1, ca. 1870s. Hand painted and
signed by amateur artist Edwin Heyska. $400-$600.

Cider Pitchers

Cider pitchers were used to serve cider, juices, and sometimes lemonade. The difference between a cider pitcher and a tankard is the size. Pitchers run 5" to 6.5" tall, are more squatty than the tall elegant tankard, and have substantial handles. Pitchers decorated in the factory have roses, fruit, berries, or some type of pattern as the design. Pitchers painted by the amateur artist can be seen with flowers, fruit, grapes, apples, berries, and almost every type of design. If a woman of wealth wanted a complete matching set, she could purchase the blanks (and hand paint them to her taste) or purchase a complete set from a fine department store that would include a cider pitcher with matching mugs and a tray. A set of this magnitude and ostentation would look fabulous on the Victorian's sideboard or in any home today.

Cider pitcher sets include the matching mugs and tray. Mugs are more delicate than those accompanying a tankard and are 2.5" to 5" tall, with or without handles. Due to the fragility of porcelain, however, many of the mugs have not survived. A cider pitcher will cost several hundred dollars while a rare set, including the pitcher with matching mugs, is valued at around a thousand dollars.

Cider pitcher, 9.5" tall, hand painted in the factory. Underglaze factory mark in green, T&V Limoges France, Tressemann & Vogt Mark 7, ca. 1892-1907. Overglaze decorating mark in red/purple, Tressemann & Vogt Mark 15. $495-$595.

Cider pitcher, 10.5" tall, factory decorated and artist signed "Roby." Underglaze factory mark, T&V France, Tressemann & Vogt Mark 5a, ca. 1892-1907. Overglaze decorating mark in red/purple, Tressemann & Vogt Mark 15. $650-$1,000.

Cider pitcher, 6.5" tall, with six matching 3.5" tall cups. Hand painted by amateur artist E.Miler. Underglaze factory mark in green, J.PL. France, Pouyat Mark 5, ca. 1891-1932. Set: $900-$1,300.

Cider pitcher, 10" tall, hand painted by amateur artist with roses and raised enameling. Underglaze factory mark in green, WG&Co., Guérin Mark 3, ca. 1900-1932. $495-$595.

Cider pitcher, 6.5" tall, with eight matching 2.5" tall mugs/cups. Hand painted with lemons by amateur artist I.L. Brunner and dated 1912. Underglaze factory mark in green, Limoges, W.G.&Co., France, Guérin Mark 3, ca. after 1900-1932. Set: $900-$1,200.

Cider pitcher, 6.5" tall, with six matching 4.25" tall cups. Hand painted by an amateur artist who did not sign, but dated the pitcher "9/29/13." Underglaze factory mark in green, B&Co., France, Bernardaud & Co., Mark 1, ca. 1900-1914. Set: $1,000-$1,500.

Coffee Pots

Americans love coffee, but during the Victorian era it would have been blasphemy to serve coffee out of one's beloved teapot. A porcelain coffee pot is more ovoid in shape than a chocolate pot or teapot and can range in height from 7.5" to 12.5". The spout will be closer to the base of the pot and straighter than a teapot spout. This coffee pot design was done specifically to allow the coffee grounds to sink to the bottom, with clean coffee being left in the rest of the pot. Sometimes collectors are confused as to whether a pot is a tea or a coffee pot. This confusion comes from the fact that iced tea was sometimes served in coffee pots. Dorothy Kamm, a well known china painter and author of *American Painted Porcelain*, cites several nineteenth century china catalogs that listed what looks like a coffee set as a tea set for iced tea.

Coffee pots on matching trays with a creamer and sugar are very desirable and useable today. Placed on the dinning room table, factory decorated pots that match or coordinate with a dinnerware set make the tabletop look most elegant. Family dinning and formal Sunday dinners may be a thing of the past, but what fun to get back to the basics, enjoy your family and friends, and serve them a delicious cup of coffee from a beautiful and still functional Limoges coffee pot. Individual coffee pots can be purchased for $200 to $500, with a set running several hundred dollars depending on its completeness.

Sometimes mistaken for a tea set, this would correctly be considered a coffee pot, due to placement of the spout. Underglaze factory mark in green, W.G.&Co., France, Guérin Mark 2, ca. 1891-1900. Set: $900-$1,500.

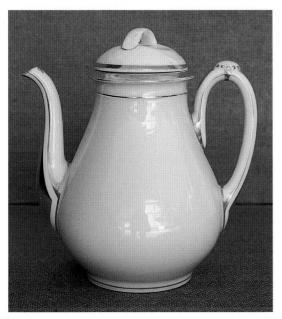

Old Wedding Band coffee pot, 11" tall. H&Co., Mark B incised on the bottom, ca. 1865. $175-$250.

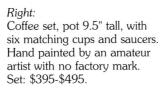

Right:
Coffee set, pot 9.5" tall, with six matching cups and saucers. Hand painted by an amateur artist with no factory mark. Set: $395-$495.

Coffee pot, 9.5" tall, hand painted by an amateur artist. Underglaze factory mark in green, Haviland & Co., Mark F, ca. 1876-1889. $295-$395.

Coffee set, pot 9.5" tall, with matching sugar and creamer, tray, and cake plate hand painted by an amateur artist "ATK." Underglaze factory mark in green, J.P.L. France, Pouyat Mark 5, ca. 1891-1932. Set: $495-$795.

Dessert Plates

Dessert plates, tea plates, or luncheon plates typically run in size from 7.5" to 8.5" in diameter. Plates smaller in size were normally used as side plates for buns, bread, and butter. Plates 9.5" to 10.5" in diameter were normally categorized as dinner plates. Sets sold at the turn of the twentieth century came with various sizes of salad bowls, but rarely a salad plate. With the evolution of dinning habits, various uses for specific sized plates followed. Many dessert plates were painted individually or as luncheon or dessert sets. A complete dessert set is rare and would include the teapot, chocolate pot, or coffee pot, along with creamer and sugar.

Most factory dinnerware sets did not include the dessert set as part of the dinnerware set, but the dessert set was available to purchase separately. As noted in the section above on cake plates, factory decorated dessert sets consisting of a cake plate and matching dessert plates are available when antiquing today.

The amateur artist of the nineteenth and twentieth centuries could randomly select blank pieces of Limoges, creating her own distinct and unique dessert set. It was not as unusual for an artist to have a hand painted dinnerware set that included a matching dessert set. Hand painted dessert sets are very desirable. Not only do these lovely decorated pieces look fabulous hanging on walls, but when needed they can be called into usefulness. Individual hand painted dessert plates run approximately $100, with a complete dessert set running into the thousands, especially if a chocolate pot or teapot happens to be part of the set.

Dessert plate, 9" diameter, hand painted in the factory. Underglaze factory mark in green, Limoges France, Mark 6, ca. after 1891. Overglaze mark in green, Limoges Coronet Crown, France, George Borgfeldt Mark 1, ca. 1906-1920. Factory artist signature on the front, "Roby." $295-$395.

Dessert plate, 9.5" diameter, factory hand painted and artist signed "Roye." Underglaze factory mark in green, AK over D, France, Klingenberg Mark 7, ca. 1890s-1910. Overglaze decorating mark in red, AK/CD in circle with Limoges France, Klingenberg and Dwenger Mark 9, ca. 1900-1910. $225-$275.

Dessert set, seven 9.5" plates and 14" long serving tray, hand painted and signed by amateur artist E. Miler. Underglaze factory mark in green, J.P.L. France, Pouyat Mark 5, ca. 1891-1932. Set: $995-$1,200.

Four plates from the set of six dessert plates. Underglaze factory mark, T&V Limoges France, Tressemann & Vogt Mark 7, ca. 1892-1907.

Dessert set, 9" x 14" serving platter with six 8.5" diameter dessert plates, all hand painted uniquely by amateur artist "S. Morgan." Underglaze factory mark in green, J.P.L. France, Pouyat Mark 5, ca. 1891-1932. Set: $795-$995.

Dessert sets, 9" plates with hand painted portrait and matching cups and saucers. Underglaze factory mark Haviland France and artist initials. Set: $195-$295 each.

Dinner Plates

During the nineteenth century, there were many changes in dining and etiquette habits. Dining was the main source of entertainment and Americans looked to the French for sophistication in the areas of manners, etiquette, and taste. Prior to the 1850s, food was served family style from large bowls or platters placed in the middle of the table. After the 1850s, it was fashionable to have a butler carve from a sideboard, a la Russe, arrange the plates, and have the food served by a servant. By the 1880s, New York was setting the standard for elegant and elaborate dinner parties. Serving a la Russe eliminated large serving pieces from the table, allowing for elaborate tabletops set with crystal, sterling, and linen. Eventually dining become so elaborate that guests complained of the formality and loss of hospitality.

Elaborate dining was looked upon as an event, a time to socialize and enjoy. Formal dinner parties went on all through the evening with course after course being served. Each course was served on a different plate, bowl, or dish. Fish would be served on platters accompanied by a sauce boat and matching fish plates. Meat of some form was served from special meat platters and placed on meat plates, with crescent shaped bone dishes available for the bones. Wild game, usually some type of foul, was served on game platters accompanied by matching bird plates. Ice cream, ices, and gelatins were served from an ice cream platter, along with matching ice cream plates or bowls or dessert plates. Fruits were served on fruit plates; petits fours and bonbons were served on their appropriate plates or dishes.

Plates 9.5" to 10.5" in diameter were normally categorized as dinner plates, but there was a full range of plate sizes. The 9.5" dinner plates tend to be those that were part of a fish, game, or meat set. By World War I, women were entering the workforce and the men were serving their country. By the 1920s, dining out—followed by an evening of dancing—was the rage. Large dinners and dinner parties with course after course being served were no longer in vogue. Porcelain factories began to produce dinner plates 10.5" to 11.5" in diameter so that one plate was sufficient for a single course dinner.

A dinner plate can run from $20 for a wedding band or common transfer ware dinner plate to $300-$450 for a hand painted plate with a preferred factory or a desired amateur artist. Complete dinner sets come in various price ranges from $150 to $1,000 for the wedding band or common transfer ware patterns to thousands of dollars for a complete set in cobalt blue or those with heavy gilt and exquisite hand painting. Complete sets are very rare and very desired by Limoges collectors, decorators, and individuals who want high end, unique dinnerware (which they do not mind hand washing) for an elaborate dinner party.

Six 9" cobalt plates from a set of twelve, each uniquely hand painted with a game bird. Underglaze mark in green CFH, Haviland, Charles Field, Mark 2, ca. 1868-1881, overglaze mark in red R.B. in script. Set: $2,000-$2,500.

Limoges dinner plate, 12" diameter, with thick heavy border of scrolled gold, lovely hand painted flowers in the center medallion. Pickard decorated and factory marked. Set of twelve: $2,500-$3,000.

Very unusual silver detailed 12" Limoges dinner plate. Underglaze factory mark in green, Limoges France, Mark 6, ca. after 1891. Overglaze decorating mark in red, Lanternier Mark 1, ca. 1890s. Set of twelve: $795-$1,295.

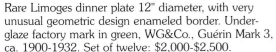

Rare Limoges dinner plate 12" diameter, with very unusual geometric design enameled border. Underglaze factory mark in green, WG&Co., Guérin Mark 3, ca. 1900-1932. Set of twelve: $2,000-$2,500.

Limoges dinner plate, 10.5" diameter, hand painted raised enamel gold paste with intricate detail, hand painted flowers inside the scribed gold. Underglaze factory mark in green, Limoges France AV enir France, G.D.&C. overglaze mark. Set of eight: $1,200-$1,500.

Dresser Sets

Elegance was part of the daily lifestyle for a Victorian woman. Sitting on a tufted chair or stool in front of an elegant dressing table, she would be accommodated by a servant or her personal nursemaid to prepare herself for the day. Beautiful hand painted dresser trays were used to preserve the tops of furniture and could be purchased in perfect sizes to display the young woman's desired pieces. Dresser sets consist of trays in various shapes from 8.5" to 14" and the accoutrements that would accompany them, generally powder or puff jars and hair receivers. Some complete dresser sets also include one or two candlesticks, a button jar, various sizes of jars and boxes, hatpin holder, pin tray, ring holder, perfume jar, talcum powder shaker, mirror, hair brush, and comb.

Complete dresser sets are very hard to find today. Many dealers have found that there is a market for specific pieces from such sets, so these pieces are sold individually. For example, hair receivers, the jars with the hole in the top of the lid that were used during the Victorian era to house actual hair prior to making hair jewelry, are very collectible. A hair receiver can run from $50 to $295, a pair of candlesticks can run $175 to $395, and brush and comb sets are $295 to $595, making the total price of a complete dresser set very expensive but each individual piece reasonable.

Limoges dresser set with undertray, pin tray, covered box, jar, and jar with feet. Complete set: $395-$1,295.

Covered powder jar on legs, 6" x 6.5", part of the dresser set. Underglaze mark in green, W.G.&Co., France, William Guérin Mark 2, ca. 1891-1900.

This ornate dresser tray, 7" x 12" in a kidney shape, is part of the set. Underglaze mark in green, W.G.&Co., France, William Guérin Mark 2, ca. 1891-1900.

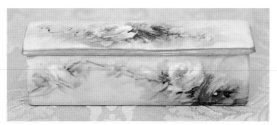

Covered box, 2" x 4.5", also part of the set. Unmarked.

Small pin tray, 2" x 4", also part of the set. Underglaze mark in green, T&V, Tressemann & Vogt Mark, 7, ca. 1892-1907.

Wonderful eight piece dresser set includes covered boxes, hatpin holder, brush set, and nail buffer. Each piece is marked with a different mark: PL France, D&Co., France, Limoges, W.G.&Co., France, ca. late 1800s to early 1900s. Sets range from $395-$1,295.

Large 9" covered dresser jar. Beautifully hand painted with woman and cherub on the front, roses along the sides of the jar, all encircled in ornate heavy gold gilt with raised enameled turquoise dots. Marked Elite, Limoges France, Bawo & Dotter, Mark 4, ca. 1896-1900. $395-$695.

Pair of 5" candlesticks. Underglaze factory mark in green, Tressemann & Vogt Mark, 7, ca. 1892-1907. $195-$395.

Limoges chamber stick. Underglaze factory mark in green, T&V Limoges France, Tressemann & Vogt Mark, 7, ca. 1892-1907. $195-$395.

Large 9" covered dresser jar. Beautifully hand painted with two women holding a garland of roses. Underglaze factory mark B&Co., France, Bernardaud & Co., Mark 1, ca. 1900-1914. Amateur artist signed and dated. $395-$695.

Ewers

Ewers run 10" to 17" high, with an average height of 12.5". Some reference sources identify the ewer as a "pitcher" but never as a tankard. Ewers are very decorative, curvaceous, and elaborate and are not as massive or heavy as a tankard. In addition, ewers were not produced with matching mugs, cups, or trays, as were tankards. An ornate ewer with the Pairpoint mark or a rare Haviland ewer can run several thousand dollars.

Ewer, 14.5" tall. Underglaze factory mark in green, W.G.&Co., France, William Guérin Mark 2, ca. 1891-1900. Overglaze factory mark in red, Wm Guérin & Co., Limoges France, ca. 1800s-1932. Factory decorated and artist signed "Leon." $700-$1,500.

Pair of ornate ewers, 15.25" tall. Hand painted by an amateur artist in breathtaking colors. Underglaze factory mark in green, W.G.&Co., France, William Guérin Mark 2, ca. 1891-1900. $900-$1,600 each.

Unusual ewer, 11" tall. Overglaze mark in red, Bawo & Dotter Mark 8, ca. 1896-1900. $800-$1,200.

Rare ewer, 11" tall, reserves hand painted with figural scenes, signed and dated "A.Nice 1893." Underglaze factory mark H & Co., Haviland Mark 11, ca 1888-1896 and "H.&Co. 1893" written in script. $2,000-$2,500.

Ferniers

Ferniers, or fern pots, are similar to jardinières in that they house plants, but originally they were intended to house only ferns. Their shape is the distinguishing feature: a fern pot is more oblong and stout than a jardinière, with the average size being 5.5" tall by 7"-9" in diameter. These ferners originally had an insert with holes. The insert acted as a liner for the pot and a drain for the plant. The plant would be placed on top of the insert so it would never be sitting directly in any accumulated water. Over the centuries, these inserts were broken or misplaced, so any type of planter with its original liner is very rare and desired by collectors and horticulturalists.

Victorians loved ferns. They loved to paint pictures of them on pieces of porcelain and raise this beloved plant in their hand painted ferners. Ferners are sought after by many collectors and their price ranges from $400-$1,000.

Ferner, 5.5" x 7", with fabulous hand painted roses and heavily gilded feet has been factory decorated. Overglaze decorating mark in green with Coronet, Borgfeldt, Mark 1, ca. 1906-1920. $550-$700.

Ferner, 5" x 8", hand painted by an amateur artist. Underglaze factory mark in green, Limoges France, Mark 6, ca. after 1891. $550-$700.

Ferner, 5.5" x 9", hand painted by an amateur artist. This entire piece is decorated with roses, including the bottom. Underglaze factory mark in green, D&C France, Délinières & Co., Mark 3, ca. 1894-1900. $700-$1,200.

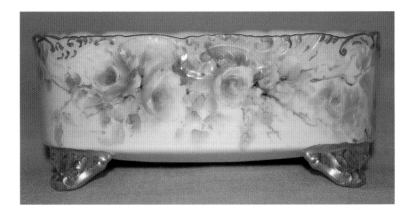

Ferner, 3" x 7.25" long, hand painted by an amateur artist. Underglaze factory mark in green, AKD France, Klingenberg, Mark 8, ca. 1890s-1910. $400-$700.

Fish Platters and Plates

During the Victorian era, dining was an elaborate event. Courses were served one after another on plates specifically designed for the type of food being served. Fish platters were over 22" long to allow for all types of fish—from cod to salmon—to be elegantly served. Complete fish sets that include the platter, sauce boat, and fish plates are very desirable and run around $5,000 if hand painted by a factory artist. Individual pieces can run several hundred dollars and if well painted are very desirable.

Large oblong fish platter, 11.25" x 22", hand painted by an amateur artist. Underglaze factory mark in green, AKD France, Klingenberg, Mark 8, ca. 1890s-1910. $795-$2,500.

Large oblong fish platter, 11.25" x 22", hand painted by an amateur artist. Underglaze factory mark in green, AKD France, Klingenberg, Mark 8, ca. 1890s-1910. $795-$2,500.

Seafood platter, 12.5" x 17", with eight matching plates and seafood dish. This set is hand painted by an amateur artist. Underglaze factory mark in green, J.P.L. France, Pouyat Mark 5, ca. 1891-1932. Complete set: $1,295-$1,500.

Lobster set includes 14.5" platter, five 10" plates, and gravy boat. Underglaze factory mark in green, Coiffe Mark 3, Flambeau studio. All pieces marked and artist signed "Dubois." Set: $2,500-$3,500.

Seafood dish, 10.5" x 7.5," is part of the set. Underglaze factory mark in green, T&V Limoges France Depose, Mark 8, ca. 1907-1919.

Four plates, each 7.5" diameter, are part of the set of eight matching plates, each hand painted uniquely by an amateur artist. Underglaze factory mark in green, J.P.L. France, Pouyat Mark 5, ca. 1891-1932.

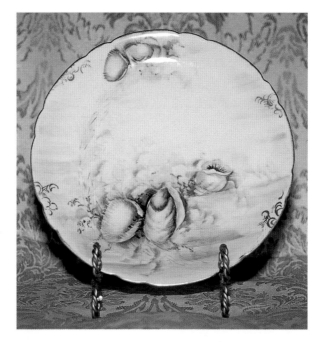

Fruit Salad or Small Punch Bowls

Conflicting descriptions in various books on porcelains make the distinction between a small punch bowl and a large fruit bowl difficult. Fruit was placed in a bowl and sometimes used as a centerpiece during a formal Victorian dinner. A master fruit bowl 10" in diameter with matching 6" serving bowls was common. This type of bowl is smaller than, and should not be confused with, a punch bowl. Also, the squatty lower bowls with feet and the bowls with a more curvaceous type of flared base were intended to house fruit. The confusion comes in when discussing the bowls that are 4.5" to 5" tall and 9.5" to 12" in diameter. Even the painting leaves us with no clues. Hand painted with fruit or berries, these bowls can be for fresh fruit or for fruit punch.

The only insight I can add comes from a discussion I had with a sterling silver dealer. Most punch bowl ladles were a minimum standard size of 12" to 14" long and would therefore be difficult to handle if used in this smaller sized bowl. On the other hand, perhaps a smaller porcelain ladle was used with this size bowl. And, although I have not seen a factory marked Limoges porcelain ladle, I have seen one with a Nippon mark. For the sake of consistency, the standard punch bowl blank that measures 4.5" tall by 9" to 9.5" in diameter could be considered a small punch bowl. And yet, what difference would it make if one were to serve fruit in one of these beautiful bowls!

Factory decorated bowl, 12" diameter, with transfer pink roses and ornate gold trim. Underglaze factory mark in green, J.P.L., Pouyat Mark 5, ca. 1891-1932. Overglaze factory decorating mark in green and pink, J. Pouyat Limoges, Pouyat Mark 9, ca. 1914-1932. $395-$595.

Factory decorated bowl, 12" diameter, with hand painted roses inside and out. Underglaze factory mark in green, Elite L France, Bawo & Dotter Mark 5, ca. after 1900. Overglaze factory mark in red, Elite Works Limoges France, Bawo & Dotter Mark 9, ca. 1900-1914. $595-$795.

Bowl, 11" diameter, hand painted by an amateur artist. Underglaze factory mark B&Co., France, Bernardaud & Co., Mark 1, ca. 1900-1914. Amateur artist signed and dated. $395-$595.

Bowl, 12" diameter, ornate gold and hand painted inside and out by an amateur artist. Underglaze factory mark in green, J.P.L. France, Pouyat Mark 5, ca. 1891-1932. $595-$795.

Jardinières

The jardinière is not only useful for housing plants, it makes a beautiful and breathtaking statement. These pieces are bulbous in shape and run from a diminutive 4" to a mammoth 18"-20" across. Some of the jardinière blanks had feet and ornate handles painted with gold gilt. Others were adorned with decorative handles in the shape of lions' or elephants' heads. Jardinières were sometimes placed on a separate stand with feet of claws or lion's paws. A base can add two to three inches to a jardinière's height. On a base, a gigantic 12" jardinière is transformed into a mammoth jardinière more than 14" tall. Both collectors and decorators find these types of jardinières very desirable as decorative pieces of art.

The Victorians were known for their love of nature and for homes filled with decorative plants. Plants acted as natural air filters, decorations for the center of a table, and a means of bringing the outside in. These much loved plants, considered members of the family, were placed in large jardinières with bases on the floor, staircases, tables, or sideboards. Smaller jardinières were used to house plants that were set in groupings on window boxes and mantels. Most of these jardinières are hand painted with some type of floral design indicative of their intended use. A few may have an abstract design with a bird or a peacock for good luck. Handles and feet may have been painted with gold gilt, dark green, or black, in dramatic contrast to the pastel colors of the flowers. Highly desired and most coveted are those hand painted with cherubs or a combination of roses and cherubs. Jardinières are priced according to their size, quality, and subject matter of the painting, and whether on a separate but matching base. Bases can add several hundred dollars above and beyond the high cost of a large and beautifully hand painted jardinière.

Jardinière, 11" tall with ornate handles, hand painted with large mums, very rare and desirable blank. Underglaze factory mark in green, D&Co., Délinières & Co., Mark 3, ca 1894-1900. $2,500-$3,000.

Jardinière, 11" tall with ornate handles, very rare and desirable blank. Underglaze factory mark in green, D&Co., Délinières & Co., Mark 3, ca 1894-1900. $2,500-$3,000.

Jardinière, 11" tall with ornate handles, very rare and desirable blank. Hand painted with fine detail of a woman and cherub. Underglaze factory mark in green, D&Co., Délinières & Co., Mark 3, ca. 1894-1900. $2,500-$3,500.

Jardinière, 8" x 12", with lions' head handles and on separate base. Underglaze factory mark in green, D&Co., Délinières & Co., Mark 1, ca. 1870s. $3,500-$4,000.

Reverse of the woman and cherub jardinière.

Rare Limoges jardinière blank on original base. Both pieces marked in green, CM in a triangle with LIMOGES FRANCE DEPOSE, ca. early 1900s-1930s. $3,500-$4,500.

Jardinière, 8" x 10.5", with elephant head handles and on separate base. Underglaze factory mark in green, D&Co., Délinières & Co., Mark 1, ca. 1870s. $2,500-$3,000.

Same blank as the jardinière on the base, but this one does not have a base and is not marked. $2,000-$2,500.

Jardinière, 11" x 12", on unusual separate base. Underglaze factory mark in green, D&Co., Délinières & Co., Mark 1, ca. 1870s. $2,500-$3,000.

Massive jardinière, 12" tall, with hand painted wisteria. Underglaze mark in green, D&Co., Mark 3, ca. 1894-1900. Jardinière with base, not pictured: $2,500-$3,000.

Lamps

In 1750, Benjamin Franklin introduced the world to electricity. It was another 150 years before there was a need for a standard type of lamp using this new form of energy. Factory produced nineteenth century Limoges porcelain lamps were the oil burning type of lanterns fashioned after the familiar oil lanterns made of glass. Oil lamps were tall and thin, with a cylinder type of base, and a bulbous cavern that held whale or other types of oil for burning. Today, most nineteenth century oil lamps have been converted to electric, hopefully while maintaining the integrity of the porcelain. By 1910 and pre-World War I, most homes had electricity and began using the type of lamp with which we all are familiar.

While there are many examples of Limoges lamps, most of them are believed to have been made out of a vase blank and then professionally wired and placed on a base. Limoges oil lamps in their original condition are very collectible and are sought after by Limoges collectors as well as lamp and lantern collectors. Lanterns and vases that have been converted are also coveted by collectors and decorators. A factory created lamp, hand painted and artist signed from a factory such as the Pickard factory, will bring up to a thousand dollars.

Fabulous 24" tall lamp, artist signed E.Miler. $800-$1,200.

Beautiful hand painted lamp, 24" tall. Fabulous new lampshade from Lamp and Shade World, Saugus, Massachusetts. $800-$1,200.

Massive Limoges lamp, 26" tall. Underglaze mark in green, T&V Limoges France, Tressemann & Vogt, Mark 7, ca. 1892-1907. $800-$1,200.

Lamp, 22" tall, converted from vase. $800-$1,200.

Original oil lamp, marked under the glaze, D&Co., France, Délinières, Mark 3, ca. 1894-1900. $1,200-$1,500.

Small 7" tall lamp. Beautifully hand painted, with porcelain base. Underglaze factory mark in green, J.P.L. France, Pouyat Mark 5, ca. 1891-1932. $600-$800.

Bulbous lamp, 23" in circumference, hand painted with poppies. Underglaze factory mark in green, W.G.&Co., France, Guérin Mark 2, ca. 1891-1900. $800-$1,200.

Beautiful hand painted lamp, 13.5" tall, with lady and cherubs. Underglaze factory mark in green, T&V France, Mark 5a, ca. 1892-1907. Converted from a vase: $600-$800.

Paintings on Porcelain

Large painting on porcelain, 26" x 22" in original frame. Beautiful portrait of a woman and two children, inherited by an Andover, Massachusetts family and thought to be hand painted by their great-grandmother. Museum quality, unsigned, marked on the back T&V Limoges France, Tressemann & Vogt Mark 7, ca. 1892-1907. $4,800-$6,800.

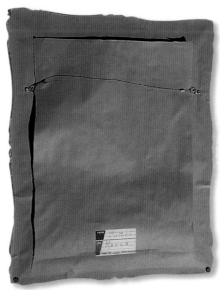

The author cut open the paper backing to authenticate markings. On the brown back is a label reading from "Mother" to "Marud."

There are many beautiful tiles produced in England, Germany, and America that were used as fireplace surrounds or have been framed and sold as pieces of art. Through my research, visits to France, and speaking with several porcelain experts, I am not aware of any Limoges factories ever producing actual fireplace surrounds. But, as shown in my first book, *Living With Limoges*, there *were* many flat pieces of porcelain in various sizes that were produced specifically to be decorated and framed as pieces of art. In addition, there have been several examples on display in the Boston Museum of Fine Arts and in museums and art galleries all over the country.

Many of the pieces of art on porcelain are marked "KPM" (produced in the Kings Porcelain Manufacturing factory in Germany) and are very valuable. Limoges paintings on porcelain are marked with one of the factory marks shown in the Limoges Marks section of this book. Many of these pieces of porcelain have "T&V Limoges France" marked on the back. Most of the paintings have been done

Mark on the back of painting on porcelain: "T&V LIMOGES FRANCE."

by one of the thousands of amateur artists of the Victorian era and are reflective of the time. Paintings of religious scenes, women, children, cherubs, and flowers are the most common, followed by scenes of nature and paintings of popular cities such as Paris and Venice. Keep in mind that these artisans, although trained in a factory or school, could paint these pieces as uniquely as their own imaginations would permit.

In *Living With Limoges*, several paintings on porcelain with a Middle Eastern or Persian theme are shown. The Victorian artist depicted these scenes in a very romantic way, reflecting the Victorian's sense of intrigue with far off places of travel. Paintings on porcelain are unique, one of a kind items, painted by an artist with a distinct and creative imagination. Reminiscent of a scene in America in 1907, the design on one—painted by an unknown artist—shows a flock of turkeys. Not the norm, but the artist may have been intrigued by the uniqueness of the bird or found that particular palate of colors pleasing to the eye.

Most of the Limoges paintings on porcelain were not hand painted in the factories but exported and painted by an amateur artist. It is rare to find a painting on porcelain that has both the factory mark and the decorating factory mark, or one that has been signed by a known factory artist. It is also unusual to find a painting on porcelain that has had the decoration transferred onto the piece of porcelain and then enhanced by an artist. Large Limoges paintings on porcelain, signed by a listed artist or attributed to a particular artist, can be very expensive and run well into the thousands of dollars. But these Limoges paintings on porcelain do not command the price of a KPM painting on porcelain or plaque. Smaller rose paintings on porcelains are more common and if you can find one, will run a few hundred dollars.

Painting on porcelain, 14" x 12", hand painted with exquisite detail. Underglaze factory mark in green, T&V Limoges France, Tressemann & Vogt, Mark 7, ca. 1892-1907. $1,500.-$2,000.

Left:
Painting on porcelain, 24" x 12", hand painted in exquisite detail. Museum quality, unsigned, marked on the back T&V Limoges France, Tressemann & Vogt Mark 7, ca. 1892-1907. $2,500-$3,500.

Right:
Large painting on porcelain, 14" x 6", hand painted in the Art Nouveau style by an amateur artist. Underglaze factory mark in green, T&V Limoges France, Tressemann & Vogt, Mark 7, ca. 1892-1907. $1,500-$2,000.

Painting on porcelain, 7" x 5". Underglaze factory mark in green, T&V Limoges France, Tressemann & Vogt, Mark 7, ca. 1892-1907. $395-$595.

Painting on porcelain, 5.25" x 3.6", in beautiful frame. Underglaze factory mark in green, T&V Limoges France, Tressemann & Vogt, Mark 7, ca. 1892-1907. $495-$695.

Square, 12" painting on porcelain in original frame. Detailed painting of an English garden. Underglaze factory mark in green, T&V Limoges France, Tressemann & Vogt, Mark 7, ca. 1892-1907. $495-$695.

Painting on porcelain or plaque, unusual blank, 13.25" x 9.25". Underglaze factory mark in green, Limoges in star, Coiffe Mark 1, ca. before 1890. $600-$800.

Painting on porcelain, artist's initials and dated 1907. Underglaze factory mark in green, T&V Limoges France, Tressemann & Vogt, Mark 7, ca. 1892-1907. $1,200-$1,500.

Planters

A planter is another name used for jardinières, ferniers, and any other type of pot that was made specifically to house a plant. A planter of any type with its original insert or frog (an insert that kept a plant or flower in place) is very rare and desired by collectors. Inserts, liners, and frogs with a Limoges mark are unusual. Inserts with a mark that matches the planter are the most desired and are very hard to find. When sold individually, inserts will bring up to $100. Marked and unmarked, inserts can add several hundred dollars to the value of a planter which, if found, can be purchased for less than a thousand dollars.

Large planter, 16" tall on base. Underglaze factory mark in green, W.G.&Co., Limoges France, William Guérin Mark 3, ca. 1900-1932. $1,500-$2,000.

Large planter, 16" tall on base. Underglaze factory mark in green, W.G.&Co., Limoges France, William Guérin Mark 3, ca. 1900-1932. $1,500-$2,000.

Planter, 7.5" with 7.5" opening. Hand painted roses, amateur artist signed "Hardin." Underglaze factory mark in green, J.P.L. France, Pouyat Mark 5, ca. 1891-1932. Smaller size: $700-$1,000.

Planter, 9" tall, amateur artist hand painted with peacock and heavy gold. Underglaze factory mark in green, W.G.&Co., Limoges France, William Guérin Mark 3, ca. 1900-1932. $1,000-$1,500.

Planter, 5.5" tall, with ruffled edge. Amateur artist hand painted tulips, unsigned, although this does not affect the value. Underglaze factory mark in green, AK/France, Klingenberg Mark 5, ca. 1890s. $395-$495.

Planter, 5.25" tall, unique blank, amateur artist hand painted with pastel roses and heavy gold. Underglaze factory mark in green, T&V Limoges France, Tressemann & Vogt, Mark 7, ca. 1892-1907. $395-$495.

Planter, 5.5" tall, with matching underplate. Amateur artist hand painted chrysanthemums and signed on bottom "AOB." Underglaze factory mark in green, J.P.L. France, Pouyat Mark 5, ca. 1891-1932. $700-$1,000.

Planter, 11" tall, footed with reticulated edge, large beautiful roses hand painted by an amateur artist. Underglaze factory mark in green, T&V Limoges France, Tressemann & Vogt, Mark 7, ca. 1892-1907. $2,000-$2,500.

Plaques

Plaques were produced by many of the Limoges factories. The major difference between a charger (a piece of tableware that eventually found its way onto our walls) and a plaque is that plaques were never used on the dinner table. Instead, plaques were created specifically to be hung on the wall as pieces of art. A plaque has factory pierced holes in the back meant specifically for hanging. Some plaques have an old wire running through the holes, which is as good as new and useful for hanging your plaque on the wall. Since plaques were produced in the factory as such, almost all of them are decorated by a Limoges factory artist; it is very unusual to find one decorated by an amateur artist.

Plaques were made in sizes from 7.5"-8" in diameter up to 32" in diameter. Some are more beautiful than nineteenth century pieces of art on canvas and are painted and signed by some of the most prestigious factory artisans. A small plaque is still a bargain and, if you can find one, will run $100-$200. There are many plaques available that were decorated using the "mixtion" technique. Mixtion is a decorating technique in which a design is transferred onto the piece of porcelain and then the transferred design is embellished by an artist who hand paints the details. This results in a piece with the appearance of having been hand painted. These pieces may have an artist's signature stamped on the front and can cause some confusion when trying to determine if the piece is hand painted. Plaques such as these are beautiful and carry a reasonable price tag of around $400. The large plaques that are hand painted and have a factory artist's signature are very desirable and also very difficult to find. These pieces of art on porcelain have not kept up in value with nineteenth century works of art on canvas, but will run from $2,000 to $4,000 or more. Price variation depends on the quality and subject of the painting, the artist, and the size.

Plaque, 16" diameter. Overglaze decorating mark in green, Limoges over a crown and France, Coronet Mark 1, ca. 1906-1920. Factory artist signature on front, "A. Bronssillon." $1,500-$1,700.

Plaque, 16" diameter. Overglaze decorating mark, Coronet, Limoges France with a crown, George Borgfeldt Mark 1, ca. 1906-1920. Factory artist signature on front, "A. Bronssillon." $1,000-$1,500.

Plaque, 13" diameter, factory hand painted. Overglaze decorating mark in gray, Lazeyras, Rosenfeld, and Lehman, Mark 3, ca. 1920s. $1,000-$1,200.

Plaque, 14" diameter. Underglaze factory mark in green, torch with Limoges France, Flambeau Mark 1, ca. 1890s-1914. Overglaze factory mark in red, torch with Limoges France, Flambeau Mark 2, ca. 1890s. $495-$695.

Plaque, 13" diameter. Overglaze decorating mark in red, A&D, Limoges France, ca. late 1800s. $700-$900.

Plaque, 12" diameter, factory decorated. Underglaze factory mark in green, torch with Limoges France, Flambeau China (LDB&C) Mark 1, ca. 1890s-1914. Overglaze decorating mark in light gray green, Flambeau China, variation of Mark 4, ca. 1890s. $995-$1,200.

Left:
Plaque, 14" diameter. Underglaze factory mark in green, torch with Limoges France, Flambeau Mark 1, ca. 1890s-1914. Overglaze factory mark in red, torch with Limoges France, Flambeau Mark 2, ca. 1890s. Factory artist decorated and signed "Dubois." This particular factory artist tends to command a higher price. $1,500-$2,000.

Right:
Plaque, 12" diameter, with boldly painted rooster. Underglaze factory mark in green, Limoges France, Mark 6, ca. after 1891. Overglaze factory mark in red, Flambeau China, Mark 2, ca. 1890s. Factory artist signed "Rex." $295-$495.

Plaque, 13" diameter, one of a pair. Underglaze factory mark in green, torch with Limoges, France, Flambeau China (LDB&C) Mark 1, ca. 1890s-1914. Overglaze decorating mark in green, Flambeau China Mark 3, ca. 1890s-1900s. Factory artist signed "Coudert." $495-$695 each.

Plaque, 13" diameter, one of a pair. Underglaze factory mark in green, torch with Limoges, France, Flambeau China (LDB&C) Mark 1, ca. 1890s-1914. Overglaze decorating mark in green, Flambeau China Mark 3, ca. 1890s-1900s. Factory artist signed "Coudert." $495-$695 each.

Punch Bowls

The Victorians loved to entertain. They served punch from lovely punch bowls that would be stationed on sideboards and buffets. Sometimes two types of punch, an alcoholic and a non alcoholic punch, would be served. This accounts for a few lucky collectors today having matching punch bowls, or two bowls hand painted very similarly by the same amateur artist. The Limoges factories produced some wonderful punch bowls: large bowls with feet or on a separate base, some with a scalloped rim, and some as large as 26" in diameter. Bowls were accompanied by matching underplates or trays, plus cups or mugs. Due to the fragility of porcelain, many of the cups, mugs, and bases have not survived, or have been separated from their original bowls. Indeed, many large punch bowls themselves have not survived, making punch bowls very collectible and sought after by most collectors and decorators. Punch bowls make a grand statement in an entryway, parlor, living or dining room. These magnificent bowls make wonderful centerpieces on tables, sideboards, and countertops.

Punch bowls come in many sizes. A standard size for a Limoges punch bowl, without base, is 6" to 7.5" high with a diameter of 13.5" to 17.5". A separate base, or feet, will add 2" to 3" in height. However, various factories produced punch bowls in other sizes, from 4.5" high and 10" to 26" in diameter. One of the most beautiful punch sets is an undecorated Ranson blank, pictured on page 153 of Nora Travis's book, *Haviland China*. Two of the largest punch bowl blanks, with and without feet, were produced in the Jean Pouyat factory and are pictured in *Living With Limoges*, pages 24 and 61.

Punch cups vary as much as their respective bowls. Factories produced cups on pedestals, 2" to 5.25" tall, cups with and with out handles, and mugs. An undertray would run at least 16" to 18" in diameter, would have a lip on the edge, and would match the decoration of the bowl. A complete, matching punch set with a bowl, undertray, and cups is very desirable and, if found, will run into the thousands of dollars.

Punch bowl, 10.5" tall on base. Underglaze factory mark in green, T&V Limoges France Depose, Tressemann & Vogt, Mark 8, ca. 1907-1919. Overglaze decorating mark in red, Tressemann & Vogt Mark 16, ca. 1907-1919. Factory artist signed "Rozy." $900-$1,500.

Massive punch bowl, 8.5" tall by 15.5" diameter, hand painted by a factory artist with huge, bold roses. Underglaze factory mark in green, Limoges France, Mark 1, ca. after 1891. Overglaze factory decorating mark in blue, Imperial Limoges France with a crown, ca. 1880s to early 1900s. This bowl is hand painted by a factory artist, but is unmarked. The matching cups to the bowl did have the artist's signature, but have been sold separately. Age and markings are a factor in the value; the cups would have increased the value. $3,500-$4,500.

Inside of massive punch bowl.

Marks on the bottom of the bowl.

Punch bowl, 13.5" on separate base with matching 18" tray, hand painted by an amateur artist with ornate gilding. Underglaze factory mark in green, T&V Limoges France, Tressemann & Vogt Mark 7, ca. 1892-1907. Set: $3,500-$4,500.

Gorgeous punch bowl, 6.5" x 15.5", amateur hand painted with heavy gold gilt, includes six matching cups and tray. Underglaze factory mark in green, T&V Limoges France, Tressemann & Vogt Mark 7, ca. 1892-1907. Set: $2,500-$3,500.

Punch bowl, 5.5" x 9", ornate hand painted gold gilding on the inside with a 3" border of greenery, outside nicely done with ornate grapes. Underglaze mark in green, D&Co., Délinières Mark 1, ca. 1870s. Value based on unique and nicely done painting, size, and old mark: $1,700-$2,200.

Punch bowl, 6.5" x 13.5", uniquely hand painted sweet peas with heavy gold trim on original base. Underglaze factory mark in green, T&V Limoges France, Tressemann & Vogt Mark 7, ca. 1892-1907. $2,500-$3,500.

Inside of punch bowl.

Punch bowl, 6.5" x 14", with heavy gold gilding. Underglaze factory mark in green, T&V Limoges France, Tressemann & Vogt Mark, 7, ca. 1892-1907. $2,500-$3,500.

Tankards

Entertainment during the Victorian era was an everyday event. Afternoon teas and receptions were handled with elegance and ostentation. In place of tea, sometimes hot chocolate or lemonade would be served. At a reception, wine or ale might be the beverage of choice. A tankard with matching mugs made a lovely presentation when serving lemonade, wine, or ale at one of these events. Tankards are cylindrical in shape, have a handle, and range from 10" to 18" in height. For collectors, some of the most desired tankard blanks are the taller ones with a ruffled edge around the lip as well as those with a dragon handle. Mugs that would have accompanied a tankard as part of a set are 4" to 6" tall and are short replicas of the tankard.

Tankard sets decorated in the factory have the same factory mark, include matching mugs and sometimes a tray, and are all decorated exactly the same. Sets decorated by amateur artists are unique. The amateur artist could select any tankard, mug, or tray blank available on the market. As a result, there are many amateur decorated tankard sets with mugs that do not match the tankard exactly. If the set has a tray, it may not be a Limoges blank. Sets hand painted by an amateur artist would be painted in the same style. The artist may have placed his or her initials plus a date on the bottom of each piece.

A complete tankard set with matching mugs and an underplate or tray is very desirable. Prices run from several hundred dollars up to several thousand dollars for a complete set.

Tankard, 14.5" tall. Underglaze factory mark in green, J.P.L. France, Pouyat Mark 5, ca. 1891-1932 and old original paper label over the glaze. Factory decorated, no signature. $1,400-$1,600.

Tankard, 13.5" tall. Amateur artist hand painted with roses and heavy gold. Underglaze factory mark in green, J.P.L. France, Pouyat Mark 5, ca. 1891-1932. $1,200-$1,400.

Tankard, 15" tall, hand painted by amateur artist. Underglaze factory mark in green, W.G.&Co., Limoges France, William Guérin Mark 3, ca. 1900-1932. $1,200-$1,400.

Tankard, 15" tall, hand painted by amateur artist. Underglaze factory mark in green, T&V Limoges France, Tressemann & Vogt Mark 7, ca. 1892-1907 and overglaze Tressemann & Vogt factory Mark 16, ca. 1907-1919. $900-$1,200.

Tankard, 13" tall, berries design, hand painted by amateur artist. Underglaze factory mark in green, D&Co., France, Mark 3, ca. 1894-1900. $900-$1,200.

Tankard, 13" tall, lady and cherub design, hand painted by amateur artist. Underglaze factory mark in green, D&Co., France, Mark 3, ca. 1894-1900. Fine detail of the painting and the cherubs affect the value: $1,600-$1,800.

Teapots

"I'm a little teapot short and stout, here is my handle and here is my spout." Most of us are familiar with this childhood song, never realizing how accurate this description actually is! Teapots are squattier than chocolate and coffee pots and their shape allows for expansion of the tea leaves. A teapot's spout is also more curvaceous, making it harder for the tea leaves to make their way through the spout and into the cup.

Teapots come in many shapes and sizes, from 3.5" tall for a single cup pot to 10.5" tall for a six cup pot. Tea sets commonly came with a creamer and sugar, matching cups and saucers, and a tray. Luncheon sets would include a tea set, a matching cake or serving plate, and 8.5" diameter luncheon plates. If the set was decorated in the factory, all pieces would have the same pattern or decoration. If the blanks were purchased and decorated by an amateur artist, each set would be as unique as the individual who hand painted it. A complete luncheon set with matching tea and coffee pot, cups and saucers, chocolate pot with cups and saucers, and sugar and creamer on a matching tray is very rare and such a complete set would be very desirable.

Original watercolor, 22" x 17", by Nancy Bautzmann, featured on the cover of the Autumn 2001 issue of *Tea A Magazine*. Tea set is from the author's personal collection and is marked J.P.L. France, Pouyat Mark 5, ca. 1890-1932. Artist signed "MY" and dated "1904." $700-$900.

Tea set includes teapot, sugar, creamer, six cups with saucers, six 6" dessert plates, and six 8" dessert plates. Underglaze factory mark in green, B&C Limoges France, Bernardaud & Co., Mark 2, ca. 1914-1930s. Complete set: $1,400-$1,800.

Darling hand painted, unmarked teapot. $195-$295.

Tea set includes teapot, cream and sugar, and four matching cups and saucers. Pot has the underglaze factory mark in green, CA France Depose, Charles Ahrenfeldt Mark 6, ca. 1894-1930s. Cups and saucers are marked with the Ahrenfeldt Mark 7, ca. 1894-1930s. Set: $450-$650.

Teapot, almost 7" tall x 11" long. Underglaze factory mark in green, T&V Limoges, Tressemann & Vogt Mark 4b, ca. 1892-1907. $295-$395.

Trays

A Limoges tray as part of a set is very desirable, but these lovely, uniquely shaped pieces have become very collectible as individual pieces of art as well. Trays were placed under dresser sets, punch bowls, tankards, cider pitchers, tea-pots, coffee pots, and chocolate pots. Dresser trays run 8"-14" and come in a variety of shapes. Massive punch bowl trays run as large as 18"-24" in diameter. Individual trays can run several hundred dollars and well into the thousands, depending on the size and quality of the painting.

Large tray, 12.5" x 16", with vibrant colors and raised gold gilt. Underglaze factory mark in green, T&V Limoges France, Tressemann & Vogt Mark 7, ca. 1892-1907. $775-$975.

Large tray, 12.5" x 16", with detailed, hand painted scene. Underglaze factory mark in green, T&V Limoges France, Tressemann & Vogt Mark 7, ca. 1892-1907. $775-$1,225.

Tray, 16" wide. Underglaze factory mark in green, T&V Limoges France, Tressemann & Vogt Mark 7, ca. 1892-1907. $775-$975.

Round tray, 16" diameter. Underglaze factory mark in green, GDA France, Gérard, Dufraisseix, Abbot, Mark 1, ca. 1900-1941. $595-$795.

Round tray, 16" diameter. Underglaze factory mark in green, GDA France, Gérard, Dufraisseix, Abbot, Mark 1, ca. 1900-1941. $595-$795.

Tray, 12.5" x 8.25", hand painted by an amateur artist. Underglaze factory mark in green, T&V Limoges, Tressemann & Vogt Mark 4b, ca. 1892-1907. $595-$795.

Umbrella Stands

Limoges umbrella stands are very unique and rare. Finding an umbrella stand with a factory Limoges mark is very desirable. Umbrella stands average 18" in height, have a very large opening at the top, and are bulkier and much heavier than a vase. These large decorative pieces of Limoges are sought after by collectors and decorators alike and are priced well into the thousands of dollars.

Massive Limoges umbrella stand, 18" tall x 8" opening. No marks, amateur artist signature on the front. $2,500-$3,500.

Reverse of umbrella stand.

Vases

The vase is the most collectible of all pieces of Limoges porcelain, with the exception of dinnerware. Many different blanks—curvaceous, cylindrical, bulbous, tall, short, with handles and without—were produced in the many Limoges factories producing decorative pieces. The sizes run from short and squat to so tall that several pieces may be bolted together. Some have necks wide enough to house two dozen roses, others have thin necks that can fit only the stem of a single flower. Many of these vases were decorated in a Limoges decorating factory, and many more were decorated by amateur artists.

The Victorians loved to garden and they loved flowers everywhere. Floral designs were used in their wallpaper, carpets, dinnerware, fabrics, needlepoint—and in their china painting. Vases filled with flowers were placed daily in the entryway, parlor, formal living and dining areas, and bedrooms. Using a vase blank as if it were a canvas, they most often painted the beloved rose. The rose is ethereal, but you can find vases decorated with violets, wisteria, pansies, poppies, chrysanthemums, lilies, orchids, daisies, dandelions, portraits of women, couples, scenes, and animals. Each vase was as individual as the artist who painted it.

Today, collecting large, ornate, unusually shaped vases that are well painted, factory artist signed, and in perfect condition can be challenging and expensive. Vases of this type run several thousand dollars. But the smaller vases, which are just as lovely, are readily available and run from less than a hundred to several hundred dollars. The average price today for a beautiful 12" vase with no repairs, well painted, and marked runs several hundred to a thousand dollars or more. Buyer beware, as many broken vases are being sold, repaired, and then resold. If there is a question, a porcelain dealer in your area can always do a black light check on the piece. Keep in mind that if the gold looks too good to be true, it has probably been retouched. Gold wear on the handles and rims is normal and unless totally worn, does not affect the overall value of a vase. Some decorators and collectors prefer to have vases with gold wear receive a professional touch up. This practice does not seem to affect the value and reputable dealers will disclose this type of action prior to a sale.

One of a pair of large, 16" tall vases hand painted in the factory. Underglaze factory mark in green, P.M. Mavaleix, ca. 1908-1914. Overglaze decorating mark, Limoges Coronet France, Borgfeldt Mark 1, ca. 1906-1920. $2,500-$3,000 each.

Marks on the bottom of the vase. The underglaze factory mark identifies the factory in which the piece was produced. The overglaze decorating mark identifies the factory where the piece was decorated.

Vase, 10.5" tall, factory decorated and artist signed "Segur." Underglaze factory mark in green J.P.L. France, Pouyat Mark 5, ca. 1891-1932. $795-$995.

Vase, 14.5" tall, beautifully hand painted with cherubs and raised gold paste. Underglaze Pairpoint Limoges Mark, ca. 1880s-1900. The mark adds to the value of this piece: $2,000-$2,500.

Vase, 15" tall, hand painted with desirable design of woman and cherub. Marked Elite Limoges France, Bawo & Dotter Mark 8, ca. 1896-1900. $2,500-$3,500.

Vase, 15" tall, hand painted by amateur artist. Underglaze factory mark in green, W.G.&Co., Guérin, Mark 3, ca. 1900-1932. $600-$900.

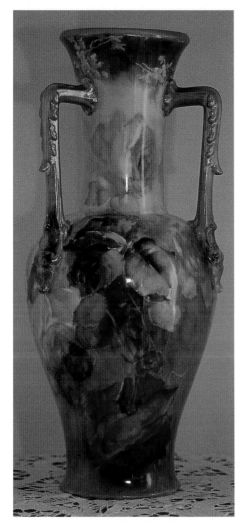

Rare and unusual three-handled vase (only two can be seen in this photograph), 15" tall. Underglaze factory mark T&V France, Tressemann & Vogt, Mark 5a, ca. 1892-1907. $2,000-$2,500.

Vase, 15" tall, with ornate handles. Underglaze factory mark in green, J.P.L., Pouyat Mark 3, ca. 1876-1890. Size, mark, and handles affect the value: $2,000-$2,500.

Vase, 12" tall, with ornate reticulation and handles. Underglaze factory mark in green, J.P.L. France, Pouyat Mark 5, ca. 1891-1932. Amateur artist signed "M.I. Hall" and dated "1902." $1,200-$1,400.

Vase, 12.5" tall, hand painted with beautiful muted colors. Underglaze factory mark in green, Limoges with a star and France, Latrille Frères, Mark 1, ca. 1899-1913. $900-$1,200.

Vase, 12" tall, hand painted with ornate detail and heavy gold. Underglaze mark in green, AK/D France, Klingenberg Mark 7, ca. 1890s-1910. $1,200-$1,400.

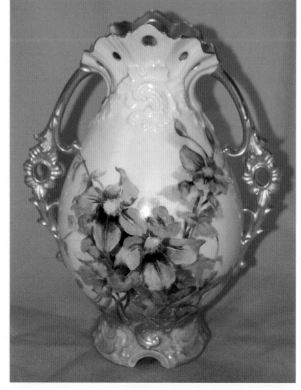

Above:
Vase, 8.5" tall, with hand painted wisteria. Underglaze factory mark in green, J.P.L., France, Pouyat Mark 5, ca. 1891-1932. $795-$995.

Right:
Mammoth floor vase, 22.5" tall, artist signed "RSCHOLZ" with raised enameling over the hand painted roses. Underglaze factory mark in green, T&V Limoges France, Tressemann & Vogt Mark 7, ca. 1892-1907. $2,200-$2,500.

Large floor vase, 17" tall, hand painted with pastel roses. Underglaze factory mark in green, B&C France, Bernadaud & Co., Mark 1, 1900-1914. $1,700-$2,000.

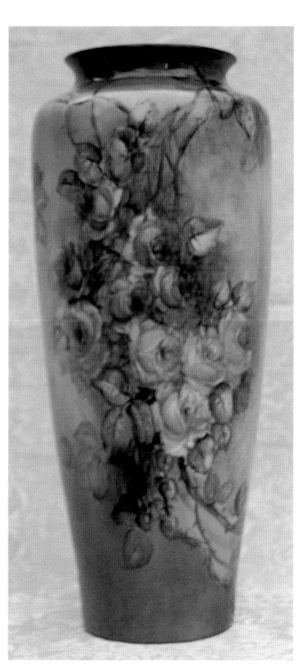

Left:
Vase, 14" tall, ornate blank with heavy gold. Underglaze factory mark in green, T&V Limoges France, Tressemann & Vogt Mark 7, ca. 1892-1907. $995-$1,200.

Below:
Vase, 6" x 9", painted in beautiful muted shades. Underglaze factory mark in green, T&V Limoges France, Tressemann & Vogt Mark 7, ca. 1892-1907. $600-$800.

Mammoth floor vase, 17" tall, unsigned. Underglaze factory mark in green, T&V Limoges France, Tressemann & Vogt Mark 7, ca. 1892-1907. $1,700-$2,200.

Cache pot, 9" tall, hand painted poppies and heavy burnished gold. Underglaze factory mark in green, W.G.&Co., Guérin Mark 3, ca. 1900-1932. $800-$1,000

Unusual vase, 7" tall, hand painted roses with raised gold gilt and intricate enameling. Underglaze factory mark in green, T&V Limoges France, Tressemann & Vogt Mark 7, ca. 1892-1907. $595-$795.

Vase, 12" tall, unmarked, attributed to the Limoges factories. This was a popular blank in the late 1800s to early 1900s and is very desired by collectors today. Many amateur artists hand painted this blank. The value is determined by condition, quality of the painting, and amount of gold. This one is hand painted and signed by amateur artist E.Miler. It is in perfect condition with heavy gold on the handles. $1,500-$2,000.

Miscellaneous Pieces

Limoges was produced in all sizes and shapes, from dinnerware to decorative pieces. Some of the many pieces include baskets, bowls, boxes, butter pats, butter dishes, candlesticks, chamber pots, clocks, compotes, cracker jars, crumb pans, dolls, humidors, match strikes, napkin holders, picture frames, salts, salt and pepper shakers, spittoons, tea strainers and caddies, tussie mussies and whiskey jugs. Even the most utilitarian piece was beautifully decorated and today may be very collectible and even viewed as a piece of art.

Rare match holder with striker on bottom. Artist signed "M.E.B. Hutchins," dated 1907. Underglaze factory mark in green, D&Co., France, Délinières & Co., Mark 3, ca. 1894-1900. $300-$400.

Rare tussie mussie (also known as a posey holder or nosegay), marked AK France, Klingenberg Mark 7, ca. 1890s-1910. $395-$495.

Cuspidor, or spittoon, 7"
x 9". Underglaze factory
mark in green, H&Co.,
underscored, Haviland
&Co., Mark D, ca. 1877.
$500-$600.

Letter holder, 6.5" tall x 8" wide. Underglaze factory
mark in green, France, ca. 1896-1900s. $275-$375.

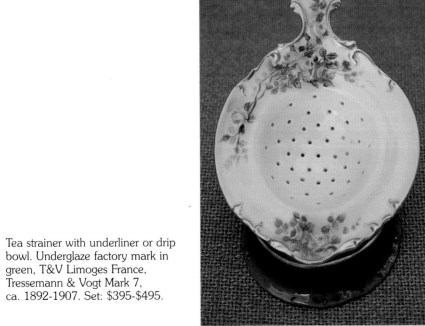

Tea strainer with underliner or drip
bowl. Underglaze factory mark in
green, T&V Limoges France,
Tressemann & Vogt Mark 7,
ca. 1892-1907. Set: $395-$495.

Inkwell with lids hand painted by amateur artist "S.M. P"
and dated "1902." Underglaze
factory mark in green, T&V France, Tressemann & Vogt Mark 5a, ca. 1892-1907. $495-$795.

Part IV
Wearing Your Limoges

Limoges brooches, buttons, boxes, and miniatures are sometimes categorized as specialty items. There are many resources for the collector of Limoges boxes, but Limoges brooches, buttons, hat and stickpins, earrings, fobs, and buckles were overlooked until my first book, *Living With Limoges*, was published. These exquisite pieces of Limoges are tiny works of art and a true joy to collect. Everyone can easily carry such small rare finds home from an antique shop, show, or flea market. These diminutive beauties are easily housed or displayed in vitrines, on shelves, on reflective plateau mirrors, in cases, and in drawers—until worn as a jewelry accessory.

Thanks to Queen Victoria, sentiment sometimes superseded usefulness during the Victorian era, 1837-1901. The Victorians wanted to combine their sentimentality for loved ones and their love of flowers with one of their favorite pastimes: china painting. These combined ingredients allowed for some of the finest small art on Limoges to be created.

By the early 1900s, china painting was nearly a million dollar industry. Due to the popularity of china painting in the United States, Limoges porcelain factories and many others imported blanks by the thousands. The United States had over 25,000 china painters, most of them women, painting all types of pieces, and these included jewelry and accessories such as brooches, buttons, belt buckles, and watch fobs. The blanks for many utilitarian accessories, as well as brooches in a variety of shapes, could be found in one of the china catalogs from the 1910s to the 1930s.

This beautiful and rare perfume bottle with gold stopper, 3" long when the chain is extended, was most likely part of a Victorian lady's chatelaine. Worn from the belt, chatelaines had watches, mirrors, perfume bottles, card and needle cases, glasses, fainting salts, and other small necessities hung from them. Most chatelaines were made of some form of metal: silver plate, silver, or gold.

Fabulous private collection of antique Limoges cobalt boxes and miniature enameled vase on a rare Pairpoint cobalt tray. There are many reference books on Limoges boxes, but until the author's first book, Limoges brooches, buttons, watch fobs, earrings, hatpins, and stick pins were overlooked.

Bottom of the perfume bottle is marked with "LIMOGES FRANCE" underglaze factory Mark 2, ca. after 1891.

Brooches

By the 1880s, wearing brooches that had portraits painted or transferred on them was in vogue. Queen Louise, Joan of Arc, Madame Pompadour, Raphael's cherub, Napoleon and Josephine, Marie Antoinette, and George and Martha Washington are some of the famous individuals who will found adorning these brooches. Keep in mind their were no guidelines for the amateur artist, who could paint anything from a beloved pet to a relative.

If a porcelain brooch or accessory does not have a backstamp from one of the Limoges factories, it is difficult to determine if it was hand painted on a piece of Limoges porcelain, on a piece that was exported from Germany or Austria, or produced here in the United States. Well into the twentieth century, the factories in Limoges were also decorating brooches in décalcomanie, the French term for transfer, specifically for export to the American market. These pieces are very common today and easily identified because most are marked on the back, "Made in France" or "Limoges France." Some are encased in gold, sterling silver, or gold and silver colored pot metal braided around the brooch. The metal may have a copper alloy, so there may be some rust or a green corrosion showing. The clasp or finding on the back is a casted, factory made clasp with a catch. You may run across a piece like this at a garage sale, flea market, or lower end antique shop and, although not considered a piece of art, it would still be a wonderful collectible.

Brooches were considered ornamental pieces of jewelry and were an important part of a Victorian woman's wardrobe. Lace pins, safety pins, and bar pins were used to keep collars, cuffs, waistbands, frills, and so on in place—due to a lack of modern laundry conveniences, such items were detachable. Tiny in size, 1/4" to 1" long, they have been mistaken as children's or infant's pins. Cuff pins were sold in pairs, while waistband pins or beauty pins—worn in place of studs on the front of the waistband or on blouses— were sold in sets of three and four. Most had intricate flowers, in breathtaking detail, either hand painted, enameled, or transferred onto the porcelain. Today, it is very rare to find a complete set. Finding pieces that were part of a set is more common and these individuals are worn today as brooches.

Collectors today can easily begin a fabulous collection of brooches, as the prices are reasonable—a fraction of what would be paid for larger Limoges pieces. The pieces are appealing, can be worn like any accessory, fit easily into a favorite Limoges box, or make a tiny art vignette on a tabletop. Prices are based on the uniqueness of shape and subject matter, detail and beauty of the painting, amount of gilt, and overall condition. Keep in mind that the older, nineteenth century brooches are very valuable if painted in great detail by a factory artist, especially with portraits of famous individuals.

Nestled on a beautiful piece of antique lace is this rare cobalt blue, heart shaped brooch, 1.75" x 2", in perfect condition, with hand painted lily and water-scape. $125-$200.

Beautiful heart shaped portrait brooch, 1.25" x 1.25", has beautiful raised paste gold dots around the border of the portrait. Portrait pins were in vogue during the Victorian era, specifically in the 1880s. This china painter paid exquisite attention to detail, making the Victorian lady look lifelike. $125-$200.

Large heart shaped brooch, 2.5" x 2.75", decorated with a combination of hand painting and transfer. The portrait is a transfer embellished with enamel, while the raised gold paste that forms the medallion and scrollwork is all hand painted. Tiny roses are hand painted inside the scrollwork. The bezel is 14 carat gold filled and hand carved with ornate roses. This piece has been in a New England family for several generations and was offered for sale in 2001 to Limoges Antiques Shop. $295-$395.

Oval, 1.75" x 2" hand painted brooch of a woman and cherub. Fashioned after Raphael's cherub, no detail is overlooked. The porcelain is set in a 10 carat gold mounting with the old "c" ring clasp indicative of jewelry from the late nineteenth to early twentieth centuries. $495-$595.

Large oval shaped brooch, 3" diameter, is set in sterling silver. Marked on the back "Limoges France," this piece is also a combination of transfer and hand painting. $175-$225.

Round, hand painted portrait brooch, 1" diameter. Hand painted gold border is painted over the glaze and embellished with raised enamel blue dots. $195-$250.

Gigantic portrait brooch of Queen Louise, almost 4" long by 2.5", set in a bronze mounting with a replacement finding or pin back. Artist signed on the front right "T.Dgt." and front left "Lyise von Preish 12." Embossed numbers on the back "16." The large size of the piece and the collectibility of Queen Louise of Prussia memorabilia add to the value of this brooch. $495-$695.

Unique diamond shaped brooch is 1.25" long. Hand painted, embellished with raised gold paste and enameled dots, with original back and findings. $125-$175.

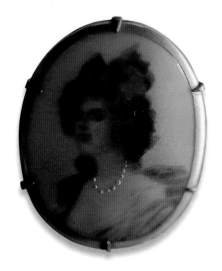

Oval brooch, 1.25" diameter. Hand painted "painted lady" with ornate detail is a bit provocative, which was the norm during the era. It was inappropriate to show off one's legs, but a plunging neckline was the fashion. $150-$175.

Oval, 2.75" brooch, has raised gold scrollwork in the burnished gold around the edge of this well painted portrait brooch. $175-$225.

Round, 1.2" hand painted portrait brooch. $125-$175.

Oval, 1.25" brooch. On smaller brooches like this, it is difficult to tell if a piece is hand painted without using a jeweler's loop. It was very common for a factory to produce these brooches using decals or a mixed process of transfer and hand painting. This portrait is hand painted. $125-$175.

Oval, 2.75" brooch, with hand painted beautiful young maiden. Burnished gold surrounds the edge and raised enamel dots represent the lace on the bodice of her dress. $175-$225.

Oval, 2" brooch, set in a detailed 14 carat bezel. This Victorian lady is exquisite. The attention to detail is evident in her hair ornaments, her curls, and the rose at her breast. Embossed numbers "29" and the porcelain is marked "CFH/GDM France." $395-$495.

Small, hand painted portrait brooch, barely 1" in diameter. $125-$175.

Oval, 1.75" brooch. Hand painted silhouette of a ship. $50-$75.

Round, 1.5" brooch. Burnished gold with raised gold paste, hand painted with light pink and burgundy roses. $100-125.

Oval, 1.25" brooch. Hand painted in exquisite detail are three pink roses and one burgundy rose. The background shading and detail in the leaves determine the value of this brooch. $100-$125.

Large oval, 2.25" brooch. Hand painted pink roses are enhanced by raised gold paste scrolling with enameled raised blue dots. $125-$175.

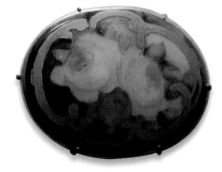

Oval, 1.75" brooch. Hand painted with two light pink roses (meaning beauty) and one burgundy rose (meaning unconscious beauty). $75-$95.

Oval, 1.5" brooch. Burnished gold with raised gold paste, hand painted with one yellow rose (meaning decreasing love and jealousy) and two burgundy roses. $100-$125.

Oval, 1" brooch, with original brass backing and "c" clasp. Hand painted in fine detail. $75-$100.

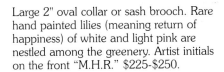

Large 2" oval collar or sash brooch. Rare hand painted lilies (meaning return of happiness) of white and light pink are nestled among the greenery. Artist initials on the front "M.H.R." $225-$250.

Large oval 2.25" brooch. Thick raised gold paste scrolls covered with burnished gold, the size, and the detailed hand painting make this brooch valuable. $200-$225.

Large 2.5" oval brooch set in ornate brass frame. Hand painted with violets (meaning faithfulness and modesty) and greenery. $250-$300.

Oval, 1.75" brooch. Hand painted with roses and white enamel highlights on flower petals, burnished gold around the edges. All of these miniature pieces of art are from a private collection and all but this one are in perfect condition. The collector could not turn down this brooch because the painting was so beautiful, but the tiny chip on the edge of the porcelain affects the value. $75-$100.

Huge oval 3.2" brooch encased in beautiful frame, ready to wear. Hand painted with ruby roses on a black background. $200-$225.

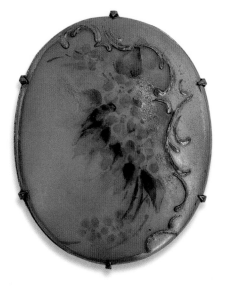

Large 2.25" oval brooch. Decorated with forget-me-knots (meaning true love and loving remembrance) and greenery. Border is thick raised gold paste with ornate scrolls. Perfect, mint condition. $250-$275.

Oval, 2" brooch. Decorated with violets and greenery in exquisite detail. Burnished gold rim. $175-$200.

Round, 1" brooch. Violets and greenery on a yellow background. $20-$40.

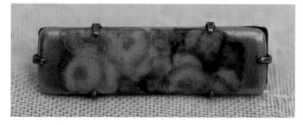

Rectangular, 1.5" bar pin. Hand painted in the Monet style with burnished gold edges. $45-$75.

Tiny, 1" bar pin for securing lace collars and decorative accessories. Hand painted tiny flower with white enamel outlining the flower. $20-$40.

Large, crescent shaped 2.5" pin. Hand painted with forget-me-knots (meaning true love and loving remembrance) and burnished gold tips. $50-$75.

Crescent shaped, 1.5" pin. Decorated with a water scene and water lily and embellished with white raised enameling. Burnished gold tips in perfect condition. $40-$75.

Bar pin, 2" long. Hand painted with a single elongated daisy (meaning innocence and beauty). Gold wear on the tips from excessive use. $20-$40.

Fobs, Stickpins, and Hatpins

Watch fobs, stickpins, and hatpins, although rare to find, were also made of porcelain and hand painted in different variations. Watch fobs were placed on clothing at the chest, so they are often in the shape of a heart. Many have been misplaced and most do not come with the appropriate or matching watch, making a hand painted Limoges watch fob with original watch very collectible. Hatpins measure 4-1/2" long and were used to securely hold a hat in place. Hatpins have become very collectible, and with the demand exceeding the supply, they have been reproduced—thousands are currently flooding the market. It is easy to mistake a hatpin made from a button for an authentic antique hatpin. These beautiful buttons may be antique, but if converted to a hatpin should be priced well below $50, versus an antique porcelain hatpin that will run several hundred dollars. Again, it is "buyer beware," and purchasing from a reputable dealer will ensure that you are getting what you desire.

Rare Victorian watch fob in the shape of a heart is decorated with hand painted forget-me-knots and has original 10 carat pin. $100-$125.

Rare stick or scarf pin, 1.25" with 3" shank. These pins were used to secure clothing at the neck, breast, or waist. Hand painted with forget-me-knots. $50-$75.

Heart shaped stick or scarf pin is very desirable. Roses hand painted in exquisite detail are surrounded by a raised gold paste with scrolls and dots and tiny turquoise enameled dots that look like jewels. Porcelain heart is less than .5" with a 2" shank. The collector paid $250 for this beautiful and unusual piece. $125-$250.

Round 1" porcelain hatpin with 9" long shank. Decorated with George and Martha Washington using the transfer ware method. The rare set includes matching buttons. Set: $195-$225.

Stick or scarf pin, 1.25" with 3.2" shank. Hand painted with roses and burnished gold all around the edge. $50-$75.

Top of hatpin, 1.5" diameter, 8" shaft. Decoration is transfer of a young woman. $195-$225.

Top of hatpin, 1" square, 8" shaft. Decoration is transfer of a woman, embellished with scrolled, raised gold paste. $195-$225.

Top of hatpin, 1.1" square, 8" shaft. The ornate decoration of a woman is a decal. $195-$225.

Ornate pair of Victorian earrings, 3.5" long with round, 1" piece of porcelain inset into the metal. Intricately hand painted deep red roses (meaning bashful shame) with forget-me-knots and greenery. $295-$325.

Buttons

Buttons were a common form of porcelain hand painted by American china painters. These functional pieces of art are very inexpensive and make a great collection. Manufactured buttons came in sets of three, but the amateur artists could paint sets in any number desired. Women's dress and blouse buttons or studs were worn with the stud end inside the garment and the beautiful hand painted top showing. Buttons came in all shapes and were embellished with gold gilt, enamel, raised dots, florals, and portraits. Children's buttons emulated those of the adults, but were smaller in size and came in sets of four.

Some buttons have the holes in the back similar to the buttons we are familiar with today, but most are correctly considered a stud. Studs are very common and a clever collector can incorporate them into a contemporary wardrobe. Take a jacket or sweater and make a small bound hole through which the stud end can easily fit. Then secure the stud by tightening up the hole with a few stitches on either side. You will have created a unique article of clothing that is a piece of art and can easily be taken apart for cleaning.

Patriotic collection of porcelain buttons.

Victorian lace is an appropriate background for displaying buttons from the same era.

Large 2.5" brooch and pair of matching buttons. All have raised gold dots and the brooch is also decorated with tiny enameled turquoise dots. Rare set: 150-$250.

Large 2.5" brooch and pair of matching buttons, 1" diameter. Rare set: $150-$250.

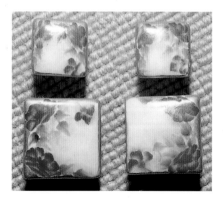

Unique set of four matching buttons in two different sizes. Set: $50-$75.

Hand painted button, .75" with raised scrolled gold paste. Artist initials on the back "JMC." $25.

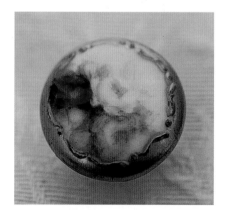

Hand painted button, .75" with raised scrolled gold paste with red, pink, and yellow roses. $25.

Hand painted button, 1" with hand painted red and pink roses and greenery. $25.

Oval button, 1" with hand painted roses, gold gilt, and tiny turquoise enameled dots that look like jewels. $25-$35.

Unique set of four hand painted buttons with different ladies painted on each. Embellished with scrolled and raised gold paste done in fine detail. Very desirable set for a porcelain and button collector. Set: $195-$225.

Large button, 1.5" diameter, part of a set. $50-$75.

Round button, 1.25" diameter, part of a set. $25-$50.

Round button, .75" diameter. Decorated with a purple pansy (meaning thoughts) with burnished gold. Beautiful detail. $25-$45.

Round button, 1" diameter. Hand painted with violets and greenery on a yellowish background. One of pair. $25.

Round button, 1" diameter. Hand painted with purple and blue flowers and greenery. One of a pair. $25.

Round button, .75" diameter. Hand painted with purple flowers. $25.

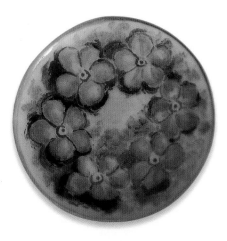

Round button, 1" diameter. Hand painted with forget-me-knots. $25.

Part V

Researching Your Limoges

Identification Marks

Trying to identify a piece of Limoges porcelain can be as simple as turning the piece over and determining if the mark on the back is one of the approximately four hundred factory marks. Each factory's distinct mark was put on a piece of porcelain prior to firing. This factory identification mark is called the **underglaze factory mark** (the mark is literally under the glaze), the **white ware mark**, or the **backstamp** and is usually green or black in color. Many of the factory marks were symbols, letters, or marks impressed, stamped, stenciled, or printed on the back under the glaze.

With many factories using letters or symbols as their underglaze factory mark, identification is *not* as simple as the back stating "Limoges" or "Made in France," as many of the marks do not include these words. Due to the McKinley Tariff Act, after 1891 it was mandatory that all pieces imported to the United States be marked "France." After 1914, it was also mandatory for all pieces to state "Made in." However, most Limoges factories did not adhere to that requirement until after 1945, especially if their identification mark included the word Limoges or France.

Some factories did not mark their pieces and it is very difficult to identify and date one of the many unmarked pieces. Keep in mind that pieces normally not marked were pieces belonging to sets such as dinnerware and dresser sets, early snuff boxes, and pieces produced during the French Revolution. Becoming familiar with the various Limoges blanks and remembering that this type of hard paste porcelain does not craze will help you determine if it is Limoges.

Once a piece of Limoges was ready to be decorated, the factory that produced the piece might also have decorated it or the piece might have been sent to another factory in the region to be decorated. The decorating factories each had their own mark that was placed over the glaze. This mark was thus named the **overglaze decorating mark**. (If you run your finger over this mark you can feel it.) Although there is always the exception, most decorating marks come in a color other than "black" or green, such as red, blue, or purple. This mark is usually much clearer and darker in color than the underglaze factory mark. Determining if your piece was decorated in the factory is thus easy if you have a double backstamp, i.e., two marks on the back: the underglaze factory identification mark and the overglaze decorating mark.

On some pieces of Limoges, there may be three marks: the underglaze factory identification mark (identifying the factory that produced the piece), the overglaze decorating mark (identifying the factory that decorated the piece), and the French exporter's mark, or the **import mark**. Import marks are usually easy to identify, as they specifically state the retail department or jewelry store that ordered a piece or complete set to sell to the American public. Some confusion is possible because the import mark was sometimes used in place of the factory decorating mark, but such pieces were decorated in one of the factories in Limoges. Examples of several retail importers whose name may appear on the back of a Limoges piece are Bailey, Banks and Biddle, Philadelphia; Tiffany's, New York; and Wanamaker's, Washington, D.C.

Factory identification mark, usually green or black. Known as the "underglaze" mark, this mark is literally under the glaze; if you run your finger over it, you cannot feel it. Factory identification marks may be letters, symbols, or words, but some factories did not include the word "Limoges" or "France."

A piece of Limoges with the underglaze factory mark and the overglaze decorating mark. This piece also states "hand painted," although few factory hand painted pieces will be identified as such.

Overglaze decorating mark, usually red, purple, or blue. This mark identifies the factory that decorated the piece of Limoges. You can feel this mark if you run your finger over it, as it is applied "over the glaze."

Sample of an import mark specifically for the Haviland & Co., Limoges factory. Some import marks identify a specific store or family which imported the pieces. This mark is also "over the glaze" and is not to be confused with the decorating mark.

Another example of an export/import mark.

French Factory Decorated and Known Factory Artists

Some of the most desired pieces of Limoges are those that were factory decorated and signed by a particular artist. A piece of Limoges porcelain hand painted in the factory would be easy to identify if it simply stated "hand-painted" or if a factory listed artist signed the piece on the front. Without an overglaze decorating mark or a listed French artist signature, however, confusion is easy and precise dating of a piece is difficult. Nonetheless, most experienced Limoges collectors are able to identify pieces that were professionally factory decorated by recognizing the distinctive styles attributed to the many factory artists.

Each artist's signature is unique. Within individual signatures, however, the flamboyant script of the time can make it very difficult to discern some of the letters in the signature. Indeed, reference books on Limoges may spell artists' names in several different ways. In studying the various signatures, I have used my jeweler's loop to distinguish between a letter, a curve, or an extra brush stroke. Below is a list of signatures (with their spellings as accurate as possible) that are associated with artists working in the French factories, along with the subjects they are known to have painted. Following the list are several examples of artists' works and their signatures.

Artist Name	Subjects Painted
Asselineau	Flowers
Alix	Fruits
Andre	Florals on plates
Arvy	Scenes
Barbeau, E.	Flowers
Barbet	Fruit
Barin, J.	Art Nouveau florals and scenes
Baumy	Women, game birds
Bay	Flowers
Bazanan	Fish, flowers
Berg	Birds
Berton	Flowers, scenes
Beyrnad, A.	Flowers
Bronssillon, T. A.	Dark florals
Brisson	Fish
Canvi	Game birds
Chamel	Flowers
Chausse	Flowers
Cibot	Portraits, cherubs
Coudert, L.	Cavaliers, domestic and game birds, animals, dogs, cats, rabbits, flowers
Damet	Flowers
Dubois	Scenes, animals, game birds, fish, portraits
Duca	Fish
Dus	Flowers
Dusay	Animals
Duval	Game birds, scenes, berries, florals, fish

Artist Name	Subjects Painted
Emile	Vellum scenes
Faynaud	Birds
Fiseier	Flowers
Furlaud, E.	Figural scenes
Gayou	Figural scenes
Genamaud	Game birds
Gex	Florals
Gilbert	Enamel flowers
Golis, Y.	Animals, scenes
Habemert	Flowers
Helene, C.	Figural scenes using "mixtion" technique
Henria	Dark florals
Janat, A.	Vellum florals
Jean, L.	Flowers
Joie, H.	Flowers
Jubal	Flowers
Kow, G.	Portraits
L.B.G.	Flowers
Lamour	Flowers
Lancy	Figural scenes
Lapin	Fruits
Laurent	Scenic plaques
Lafort/Lefort/Lefoit	Flowers
Le Pic/Le Pie	Cavaliers, monks, women
Leon/Leone/Leona	Flowers
Leroussaud	Flowers
Leroy	Flowers
Levy	Fish
Luc	Cavaliers, game birds, Indians, women, fruit, Art Nouveau flowers
Luz	Figural scenes
Lyra	Art Nouveau style, scenes
Magne	Flowers
Marcel, N.	Game birds
Marsal	Flowers
Martha	Art Deco style berries
Mary	Large flowers
Max	Game birds, scenes, Art Deco designs, flowers
Maxi	Game birds
Melo	Game birds, fish

Artist Name	Subjects Painted
Moly	Flowers
Morsey, J.	Dark berries, florals, game birds
Mullidy	Florals with heavy gold
Murray, J.	Flowers
Murville	Figural scenes, portraits
Naillet	Fish
Nanet	Florals
Naudin, M.	Large pink roses
Nice, A.	Figural
Niox	Scenes using "mixtion" technique
Noryl	Game birds
Parasil, R.	Scenes
Patllet/Paillet	Figural scenes
Paula	Florals
Petit	Figural scenes
Planehay	Fruit
Poujin, F./R.	Flowers
Pradet	Wild animals, scenes
Puisoyes/Puisoyer	Game birds, flowers
Ragoll	Flowers
Rene	Game birds, fish, florals, fruit, scenes
Rex	Florals
Riguel	Art Nouveau style, poppies
Roby	Florals
Roche	Scenes
Rory/Roye/Rozy	Scenes, flowers
Rosier, C.	Animals, game birds
Rousnet/Rousset	Scenes, florals
Sandoz, E.	Flowers, designed unusually shaped pieces
Sanstre, A.	Mythological figural scenes
Segur	Florals
Sena	Game birds
Soustre, J.	Portraits
Tharard	Fish
TOG	Animals, scenes
Triple	Portraits
Valentine	Figural scenes using "mixtion" technique
Vidal, E.	Scenes, seascapes
Wallestirz, P.	Seascapes
Yarin, J.	Women

Plaque, 13" diameter, hand painted and artist signed "Chausse."

Plaque, 18" diameter, hand painted and artist signed "A.Bronssillon."

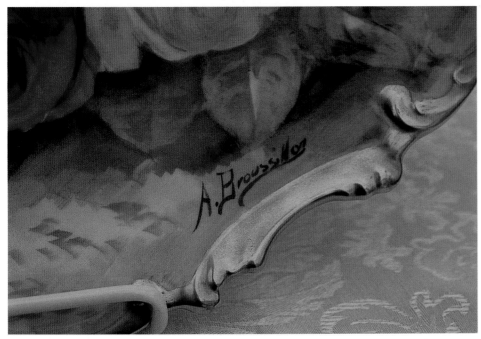

A.Bronssillon signature.

Chausse signature.

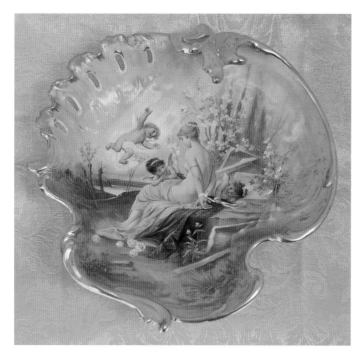

Plaque 14" diameter, hand painted and artist signed "L. Coudert."

Beautiful portrait bowl with cherubs, hand painted and artist signed "Cibot."

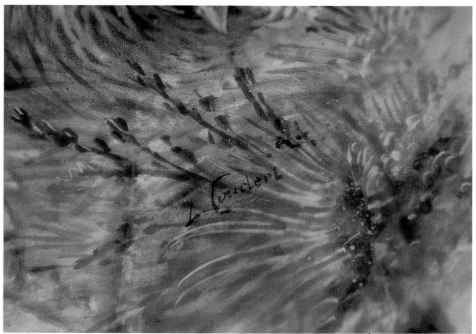

L. Coudert signature.

Cibot signature

Huge, 18" diameter plaque, hand painted and artist signed "Dubois."

Cake plate, 12" diameter, hand painted and artist signed "Lefort."

Dubois signature.

Lefort signature.

Bowl, 12" diameter, hand painted
and artist signed "Leone."

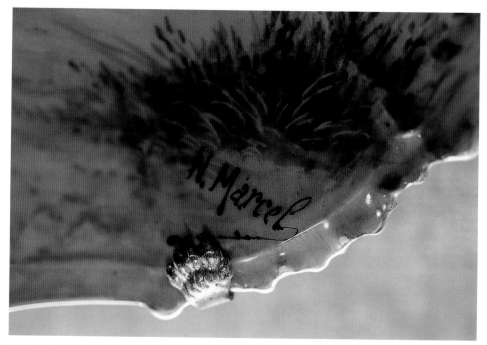

N.Marcel signature.

Leone signature.

Footed bowl with handles, 14" diameter,
hand painted and artist signed "Nanet."

Patllet or Paillet signature on portrait plates shown in the Dining section (see page 61).

Nanet signature.

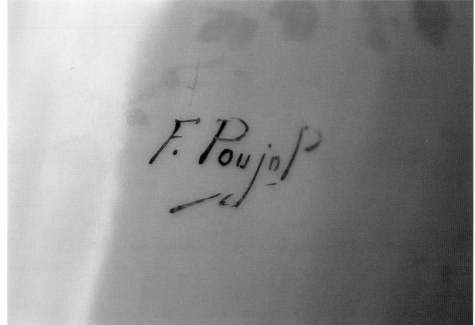

F.Poujin signature.

Plaque, 14" diameter, hand painted and artist signed "Rene."

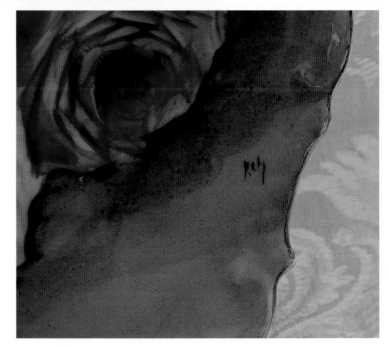

Plaque, 12" diameter, hand painted and artist signed "Rex."

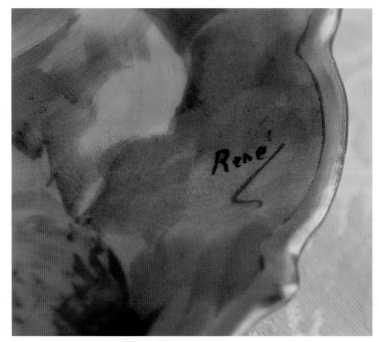

Rene signature.

Rex signature.

Plaque, 14" diameter, hand painted and artist signed "Roche."

Rozy signature on bowl shown in the Punch Bowls section (see page 170). This signature creates confusion with Rory and Roye.

Roche signature.

Bowl, 14" diameter, hand painted and artist signed "Rousset."

Tankard, 15" tall, hand painted and artist signed "Segur."

Segur signature.

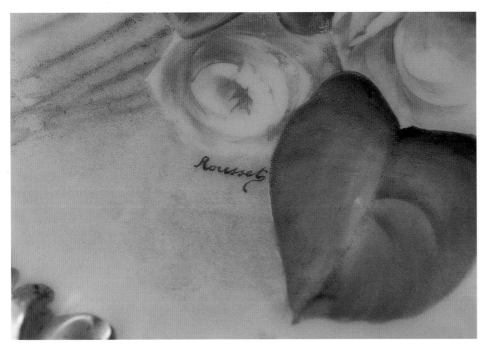

Rousnet or Rousset signature.

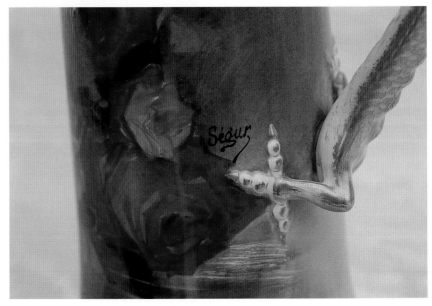

American Factory or Amateur Artist Decorated

Limoges porcelain production was at its peak during Queen Victoria's reign (1837-1901) and the Victorian era (1850-1900), when decorations with ostentation and embellishment were commonplace. Obsessed with the rose, Victorians used Limoges blanks as a means of combining their passion for china painting with their love for roses. In the mid nineteenth century, one of America's most popular pastimes was also china painting. The majority of American china painters were women who were considered amateur artists. Limited by the social mores of the time, these woman were rarely hired by American china painting factories and never achieved professional status. Women artists were not only passionate about painting, they were skilled and talented artists. These well trained and competent female artists provided Americans with a new art form and beautiful pieces of decorative and functional art.

In 1882, the Pauline Pottery Company was established in Chicago. Wilder A. Pickard's role as a salesman or "manufacturer's representative" for Pauline Pottery set the foundation for later success in his Chicago based Pickard Studios, which professionally decorated "Pickard Hand Painted China." Pickard was known for his quality decorations on porcelain done by professional male artists. In addition, he was a marketing genius and advertisements for Pickard Hand Painted China can be found in the 1910 and 1911 *Ladies Home Journal* and *House Beautiful* magazines. With popularity growing and the demand exceeding supply, imported Limoges blanks decorated in the Pickard Studios were sold in major department stores alongside pieces decorated in the Limoges factories.

By the 1900s, approximately thirty-five Limoges porcelain factories were in full production. It is documented that eighteen thousand barrels of decorated and undecorated Limoges white ware, or blanks, were being imported to the United States, sent to one of the many Chicago based mail order houses or china painting factories. In 1912, in Chicago alone, there were 49 known decorating studios and by 1916 that numbered increased to 102. This does not include the factories in New York City, Boston, Philadelphia, Cincinnati, Milwaukee, and Detroit.

American Factory Decorated

From the late nineteenth century to the early 1930s, Limoges pieces were imported blank to the United States. These blanks were then decorated either at one of the professional American decorating studios; by an artist in one of the many art studios, clubs, and affiliations all across America; or by an amateur artist in her home. The following are some of the professional decorating studios that were found in the Chicago area: American Hand Painted China Co., Burley & Co., Ceramic Artcraft Studios, Edward Donath Studio, France Studios, Illinois China Decorating Co., Kalita Studio, Keates Art Studio, J.R. Kittler Studio, C.F. Koenig Studios, LeRoy Art Studios, Luken Art Studio, Marmorstein's Art Studio, Osborne Art Studio, Pickard Studios, Pitkin & Brooks, Rivir Studios Inc., Rogers China Company, Rogers-Martini China Company, E.D. Rogers Co., Roosevelt China Studio, J.H. Stouffer Company, Tolpin Studios, Tolpin Art Studio, Illinois China Decorating Company, Progressive China Decorating Company, Delux China Studios, Western Decorating Works, White & White, Whites' Art Co., Wight Art Studio, and Yeschek Inc. For further detail, see Alan B. Reed's *Collector's Encyclopedia of Pickard China.*

Other companies or groups that decorated blanks imported from Europe were the American Hand Painted China Company, Julius H. Brauer Studio, Kay Bee China Works, Dominick Campana Studio, D.M. Campana Art Company, A. Heidrich Studios, Humboldt Art Studio, International Art

Studios, Parsche Studios, Seidel Studio, The Pairpoint Studio, and the Claremore Art Studio. Most of the American studios listed above identified themselves with an overglaze decorating mark on the bottom of the piece of porcelain. These decorating studios decorated thousands of pieces of blank European porcelain.

There were also many smaller American decorating studios, such as The M. A. Bradford Studio and the New England China Painting Shop, both located in Boston, Massachusetts. These studios held classes teaching the art of china painting and although they did not have an overglaze decorating mark, they would paint their name on the bottom of the piece.

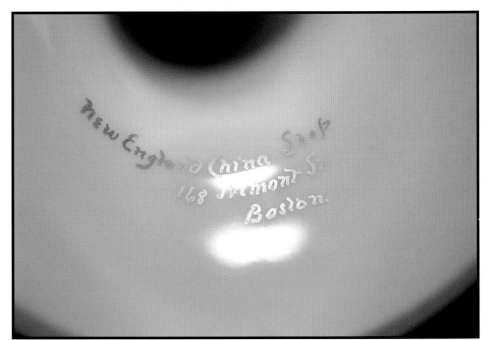

Pickard factory mark, also common in gold. The Pickard Factory was a professional American decorating factory that imported Limoges blanks, then decorated and sold them in America.

White's Art Company overglaze decorating mark. White's Art Company was another American decorating studio.

Overglaze decorating marks from two small American decorating studios in Boston.

American Factory Artists

By the turn of the twentieth century, many European factory artists had immigrated to the United States. There they began teaching the art of china painting, opening their own studios, or going to work for an American china painting factory. The American factories rushed to hire these professional male artists, thus ensuring their ability to fulfill customers' orders. This served to further solidify the socially unacceptable status already hindering the female amateur American china painters.

Many American factory artists had worked previously in a porcelain factory in Europe prior to immigrating to the United States. It was also common for American factory artists to work in several factories in the United States during their lifetime, thus having multiple studio affiliations. Some of the well known artists known for commercially decorating china in one of the American factories are: Arno, Aulich, Bardos, Beitier, Beulet, Beutlich, Bentley, Blaha, Bohman, Breidel, Burton, Buschbec, Challinor, Cirnacty, Bomyn, Corey, Coufall, Cumming, Donath, Ellsworth, Falatek, Farrington, Fischer, Gasper, Gibson, Gifford, Geoss, Griffiths, Hartman, Heap, Heinz, Hessler, Hiecke, James, Jelinek, Keates, Kiefus, Klipphahn, Koenig, Koep, Leach, Leon, LeRoy, Lindner, Loba, Loh, Marker, Miche, Michel, Miller, Motzfeldt, Nessey, Nichols, Nitcshe, Nittel, Passony, Petit, Pfiefer, Pickard, Pietrykaski, Podlaha, Phol, Post, Rawlins, Ray, Rean, Reury, Rhodes, Richter, Roden, Roessler, Ross, Rost, Roy, Samuelson, Schoenig, Schoner, Seagren, Seidel, Shoner, Simon, Sinclair, Stahl, Steiner, Steininger, Thonander, Tolley, Tolpin, Tomascheko, Unger, Vetter, Vobornik, Vokral, Wagner, Walters, Weiss, Weissflog, Wight, Yeschek, and Ziologe.

Bowl, 9" square, hand painted in the Pickard Factory, artist signed "Marker."

Marker signature.

American Amateur Artists

Americans loved porcelain. The wealthy and upper classes purchased imported decorated pieces from Europe and factory decorated pieces from one of the Limoges factories in France through mail order catalogs or from department stores such as Tiffany's. The middle classes purchased porcelain imported and decorated by one of the American china decorating studios, also through mail order catalogs and department stores such as Marshall Fields. In addition, all classes loved china painting and would purchase the blanks in order to paint their own.

Many American china painters visited Europe to learn the art of china painting. At this time, in the United States alone, there were more than 25,000 artists enjoying the pastime of china painting. Most of the amateur artists were women, as it was socially acceptable for a woman to have a talent and it showed good taste to display pieces of hand painted porcelain, considered art, in her home. The large number of amateur artists accounts for the wide variation in decoration amongst hand painted Limoges pieces.

After learning the art of china painting, amateur artists could purchase the imported blank pieces of Limoges porcelain at fine department stores and studios. Amateur artists did not discriminate against any of the Limoges factories producing these blanks—each artist chose and bought blanks based on individual interest. Blanks may have been chosen, for example, to fit into a dresser set that an artist was putting together. As a result, most dresser sets have different factory marks on each piece, though they were decorated by the same artist.

Amateur artists are responsible for most of the hand painted Limoges porcelain on the market today. The underglaze factory mark will be found on the bottom of these pieces and someplace on the piece may be the artist's signature or initials and date. However, many amateur artists did not sign or date their porcelain items, so fabulous pieces of Limoges art are often found without a signature. Accurate family records are unavailable and it is hard to identify exactly who these individual artists were. A beautiful piece of Limoges, hand painted by a family member and passed down through generations, may reach the retail market without any information on the artist. Sad, except for the fact that a piece of Limoges hand painted by an amateur American artist is sometimes more desired by collectors than pieces decorated in the Limoges factories. And, although the exact history of the artist may be unknown, the price it commands may be high and the piece may find a sacred place in a private collection or home.

Bowl with handles hand painted by an amateur artist.

Amateur artist's signature "H.E. Page" on the bottom of the bowl, also dated "1897."

Assessing and Evaluating Your Limoges

There are several factors that contribute to the price and desirability of a piece of Limoges: the factory where it was produced, the mark or marks, the age, condition, uniqueness of the blank, size, completeness of a set versus a single piece from a set, quality of the painting, and the artist's signature and date.

As stated, the factory is identified by its individual markings. Many factories are known for their simplistic designs and decorations while others are known for ornate and embellished blanks. Many of the pieces with a prewar mark are very rare and valuable and are found only in museums. Some of the best known factory marks are those from the Haviland Company. Some of the more obscure factories produced Limoges only for a very short time. These pieces are very rare and sought out by museums, clubs, and collectors.

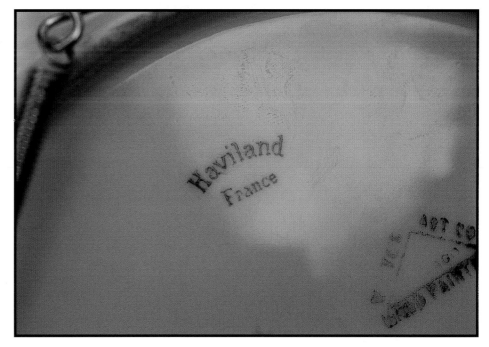

Haviland France underglaze mark.

Haviland & Co. underglaze mark.

A piece of Limoges with a nineteenth or early twentieth century mark is very desirable (see the alphabetical Limoges Marks section to help identify which mark is on the back of a piece). Add an ornate blank and a listed factory artist and you have a piece that is sought after by many collectors.

While a marked piece of Limoges is a must for collectors, so is a piece in perfect condition with no repairs. Limoges porcelain does not craze or crackle like some soft paste porcelains. A piece made in the nineteenth century will look as perfect today as the day it was produced. Hairlines, spiders, cracks, or any damage due to breakage are undesirable, but factory or firing imperfections such as pitting do not usually affect the value. In addition, stress fractures are common around the handles of mammoth jardinières and some damage on a base is overlooked. Paint touch up is undesirable, but touch up of the gold on handles and trim seems to be preferred by decorators and others who desire Limoges purely for decoration. Regilding has become a personal preference and does not seem to affect the value. Most collectors look for pieces that are as close to perfect as possible.

Desirable blanks are those that are unusual and unique, embellished with unique handles and spouts, have bases, and are either diminutive or oversized. For example, many jardinières were produced without handles and do not have a matching base. These jardinières are desirable, but not as much as the mammoth or tiny blanks that have lion or elephant head handles plus a matching base with feet. In the case of vases, which come in many shapes and sizes, the most desirable are the very unique blanks and those statuesque in size.

As noted, size is very much a factor when assessing Limoges porcelain. Large pieces of Limoges porcelain were hard to produce, fire, move, ship, and store. Small pieces were lost, as is common among covers, stoppers, tops, and lids. Finding a large, bolted, palace vase or a urn with its original stopper is very hard today and this is reflected in the price of such pieces.

Selling individual pieces out of set is often easier than selling an entire set. Thus, breaking up sets has become a common practice and increases the value and rarity of complete sets. Sets of dishes or dresser sets, for example, are commonly broken up and the pieces sold individually. There are several reasons for this practice: collectors may be looking for a particular piece in order to complete a set, some pieces are more collectible than others (salt dishes versus bouillon cups and saucers), some patterns are more desirable and the pieces sought after, and a single piece is easier to store and afford than an entire set.

The last factor noted above is the artist and the quality of the painting. My initial intent for this book was to focus on specific artists and I contacted many Limoges collectors during my research. My general finding was that collectors seem to collect a consistent subject matter—roses, portrait pieces, cherubs or game birds, for example—versus a particular artist. Many factory artists, of course, are known for painting specific subject matters. In addition, some artists have been collected widely, others are impossible to locate. The signature of a factory listed artist can increase the value of a specific piece and, if done well, these pieces are considered works of art. All Pickard factory artists seem to be sought after by collectors and tend to bring comparatively high prices. Many of the blanks painted were not Limoges, so there is a varying price range for pieces painted by the same artists, depending on the quality of the porcelain.

A few amateur artists are also starting to become well known. E. Miler, for example, is recognized for her well painted pieces featuring soft color roses. In addition, there has been a drastic increase in the price of Limoges pieces that are hand painted even by unknown American amateur artists.

Part VI

Marks

Limoges Factory Marks

Shown here are photographs of actual marks on the bottom of Limoges pieces or artist renditions of marks that were unavailable to photograph. The numbering of these marks is consistent with the published works by Mary Frank Gaston. For further research on the Limoges factories and their marks, I recommend Mary Frank Gaston's *Collector's Encyclopedia of Limoges Porcelain, Third Edition.*

Charles J. Ahrenfeldt Marks (CA), 1859 to 1969

Ahrenfeldt, overglaze decorating mark in red. 1884-1893.

Ahrenfeldt, Mark 1, in blue. Overglaze decorating mark. After 1893.

Ahrenfeldt, Mark 2, in green. Underglaze factory mark. 1894-1930s.

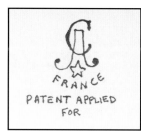

Ahrenfeldt, Mark 3, in green. Underglaze factory mark. 1894-1930s.

Ahrenfeldt, Mark 4, in green. Underglaze factory mark. 1894-1930s.

Ahrenfeldt, Mark 5, in green. Underglaze factory mark. 1894-1930s.

Ahrenfeldt, Mark 6, in green. Underglaze factory mark. 1894-1930s.

Ahrenfeldt, Mark 6a, in green, a variation of Mark 6. Underglaze factory mark. 1894-1930s.

Ahrenfeldt, Mark 7, in green. Overglaze decorating mark. 1894-1930s.

Ahrenfeldt, Mark 8a, in green, red, or gold. Overglaze decorating mark. 1894-1930s.

Ahrenfeldt, Mark 8b, in green. Overglaze decorating mark. 1894-1930s.

Ahrenfeldt, Mark 9, in blue. Overglaze decorating mark. After World War II until 1969.

Francois Alluaud II Marks (FA or AF), 1798 to ca. 1876

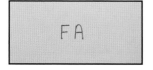

Allaud, Fancois II, Mark 1. Overglaze decorating mark. Before 1876.

Allaud, Mark 2. Overglaze decorating mark. 1876.

Allaud, Mark 3. Monogram. Before 1876.

Aluminite Mark, 1900 to 1964

Aluminite, Mark. 1920s.

Henri Ardant Mark, 1859 to early 1880s

Ardant, Henri, Mark. 1859 to early 1880s.

B.H. Mark, 1920s

Unidentified underglaze factory mark in green. Ca. 1920s.

H. Balleroy Marks, 1908 to late 1930s

Balleroy, H., Mark 1. Underglaze factory mark. 1908-late 1930s.

Balleroy, H., Mark 2. Underglaze factory mark. 1908-late 1930s.

Barny & Rigoni Marks, 1849 to 1906

Barny and Rigoni, Mark 1. 1894-1902.

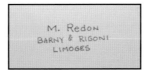

Barny, Rigoni and Redon, Mark 2. 1902-1904

Barny, Rigoni, and Langle, Mark 3. Underglaze factory mark. 1904-1906.

Barny, Rigoni, and Langle, Mark 4. Overglaze decorating mark. 1904-1906.

George Bassett Mark, 1800s to 1914

Bassett. Overglaze import mark. Late 1800s-1914.

Bawo & Dotter Marks (Elite Works), 1860s to 1932

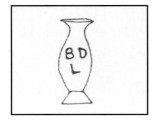

Bawo & Dotter, Mark 1, in green. Overglaze decorating mark. 1870s-1880s.

Bawo & Dotter, Mark 2 in green. Overglaze decorating mark. 1870s-1880s.

Bawo & Dotter, Mark 2a in red. Overglaze decorating mark. 1870s-1880s.

Bawo & Dotter, Mark 3 in red or green. Overglaze decorating mark. 1880s.

Bawo & Dotter, Mark 4 in green. Underglaze factory mark. 1896-1900.

Bawo & Dotter, Mark 5 in green. Underglaze factory mark. After 1900.

Bawo & Dotter, Mark 6 in red. Overglaze decorating mark. 1880s-1891.

Bawo & Dotter, Mark 7. Underglaze factory mark in green, overglaze decorating mark in red. 1896-1900.

Bawo & Dotter, Mark 8 in red. Overglaze decorating mark. 1896-1900.

Bawo & Dotter, Mark 9, in red. Overglaze decorating mark. 1900-1914.

Bawo & Dotter, Mark 10, in red. Overglaze decorating mark. 1900-1914.

Bawo & Dotter, Mark 11, in red. Overglaze decorating mark. 1920-1932.

Bawo & Dotter, Mark 11a, a variation of Mark 11. 1920-1932.

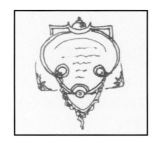

Bawo & Dotter, Mark 12, in black and brown. Overglaze decorating mark. After 1920.

Bernardaud & Co. Marks (B&Co.), 1900 to Present

Bernardaud & Co., Mark 1 in green. Underglaze factory mark. 1900-1914.

Bernardaud & Co., Mark 2 in green. Underglaze factory mark. 1914-1930s and after.

Bernardaud & Co., Mark 3 in red. Overglaze decorating mark. 1900-1930s and after.

Blakeman & Henderson Marks (B. & H.), 1900s

Blakeman & Henderson, Mark 1 in green, gray or red circle. Overglaze decorating mark. 1890s-1900s.

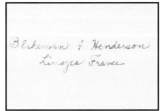

Blakeman & Henderson, Mark 2 in green. Script mark, overglaze decorating mark. Early 1900s.

Blakeman & Henderson, Mark 3 in green. Overglaze decorating mark with script mark and circle mark in green. Early 1900s.

George Borgfeldt Marks (Coronet), 1881 to 1976

Borgfeldt, George (Coronet), Mark 1 in green or blue. Overglaze decorating mark. 1906-1920.

Borgfeldt, George (Coronet), Mark 2 in green. Overglaze decorating mark. After 1920.

Jean Boyer Marks (J.B.), 1919 to mid 1930s

Boyer, Jean, Mark 1. Underglaze factory mark. 1919-mid 1930s.

Burley & Tynell Mark (B T Co.), Pre World War I

C. et J. Mark, 1800s to 1914

Chabrol Freres and Poirer Mark, 1917 to late 1930s

Chapus & Ses Fils Mark, 1928 to 1933

Chauffraisse, Rougerie & Co. Mark, 1925 to mid 1930s

Boyer, Jean, Mark 2. Overglaze decorating mark. 1919-mid 1930s.

Burley & Tyrell Company. Overglaze importing mark. 1900s-1912, pre World War I.

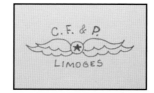

C. et J., Mark. Overglaze decorating mark. 1800s-1914.

Chabrol Freres & Poirer, Mark. 1920s.

Chapus & Ses Fils, Mark 1. Underglaze factory mark. 1928-1933.

Chauffraisse, Rougerie, & Co., Mark. Late 1920s.

Coiffe Marks, 1870s to mid 1920s

Comte D'Artois Mark, ca. 1930s and after

Creange, Henri Mark (HC), 1907 to 1914

Coiffe, Mark 1 in green. Underglaze factory mark. Before 1890.

Coiffe, Mark 2 in green. Underglaze factory mark. After 1891-1914.

Coiffe, Mark 3 in green. Underglaze factory mark. After 1891-1914.

Coiffe, Mark 4 in green. Underglaze factory mark. 1914-1920s.

Comte D'Artois, Mark. Overglaze decorating mark. Late twentieth century.

Creange, Henri, Mark 1. Underglaze factory mark. 1907-1914.

Délinières, R. Marks (D&Co.), 1860 to 1900

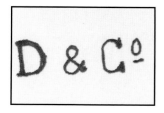

Délinières, R. (D&CO.), Mark 1 in green. Under-glaze factory mark. 1870s.

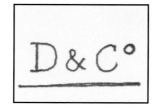

Délinières, R. (D&CO.), Mark 2 in green. Under-glaze factory mark. 1879-1893.

Délinières, R. (D&CO.), Mark 3 in green. Under-glaze factory mark. 1894-1900.

Délinières, R. (D&CO.), Mark 4 in red. Overglaze decorating mark. 1881-1893.

Délinières, R. (D&CO.), Mark 5 in red. Overglaze decorating mark in script form. 1894-1900.

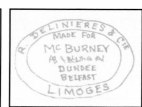

Délinières, R. (D&CO.), Mark 6 in red. Overglaze decorating mark with importer.

Flambeau China Marks (L.D.B.&Co.), late 1890s to World War I

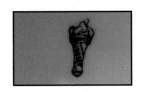

Flambeau China, Mark 1 in green. Underglaze factory mark. 1890s-1914.

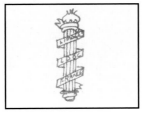

Flambeau China, Mark 2 in red. Overglaze decorating mark. 1890s, used prior to factory producing porcelain.

Flambeau China, Mark 3 in green, red, or blue. Overglaze decorating mark. 1890s-early 1900s.

Flambeau China, Mark 4 in green. Overglaze decorating mark. 1890s-early 1900s.

Flambeau China, Mark 4a, a variation of Mark 4. Overglaze decorating mark. 1890s-early 1900s.

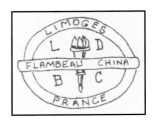

Flambeau China, Mark 5 in green. Overglaze decorating mark. Before 1914 and after Marks 2, 3, and 4.

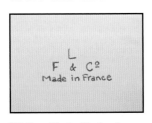

Flambeau China, Mark 6 in green. Overglaze decorating mark. Before 1914 and after Marks 2, 3, and 4.

Fontanille & Marraud Marks (F.M.), 1930s to Presentg

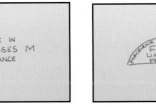

Fontanille and Marraud, Mark 1. After 1935.

Fontanille and Marraud, Mark 2. After 1935.

Fontanille and Marraud, Mark 3. After 1935.

Fontanille and Marraud, Mark 4. After 1935.

André Francois Mark, 1919 to mid 1930s

Francois, André, Mark. Underglaze factory mark. 1919 to mid 1930s.

F & Co. Mark, 1920 and after

F&Co., Mark. Underglaze factory mark. 1920 and after.

G D Mark, Early 1900s

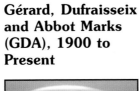

GD Mark in orange. Overglaze decorating mark. Early 1900s.

Gérard, Dufraisseix and Abbot Marks (GDA), 1900 to Present

Gérard, Dufraisseix, and Abbot, Mark 1 in green. Underglaze factory mark. 1900-1941.

Gérard, Dufraisseix, and Abbot, Mark 2 in green. Underglaze factory mark. Early 1900s.

Gérard, Dufraisseix, and Abbot, Mark 3 in red. Overglaze decorating mark. 1900-1941.

Gérard, Dufraisseix, and Abbot, Mark 4 in red. Overglaze decorating mark. 1941 to present.

Gérard, Dufraisseix and Morel Marks (GDM), 1881 to 1890

Gérard, Dufraisseix, and Morel, Mark 1 in green. Underglaze factory mark. 1882-1890.

Gérard, Dufraisseix, and Morel, Mark 2 in green. Underglaze factory mark. After 1891-1900.

Gérard, Dufraisseix, and Morel, Mark 3 in red, blue, gray, brown or black. Overglaze decorating mark. 1882-1900.

Gibus and Redon Marks, 1872 to 1882

Gibus and Redon, Mark 1. Incised factory mark. 1872-1881.

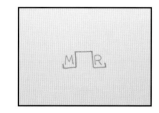

Gibus and Redon, Mark 2. Overglaze decorating mark. Prior to 1882.

G. I. D. Mark, 1910 to 1930

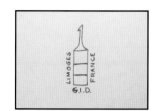

G.I.D., Mark. Underglaze factory mark. 1910-1930.

Gimbel Brothers Mark, 1930s

Gimbel Brothers, Mark. Overglaze decorating mark. 1930s.

A. Giraud Mark, 1920s

Giraud, A., Mark. Underglaze factory mark. 1920s.

Granger Marks, 1922-1938

Granger, Mark 1 in green. Underglaze factory mark. 1922-1938.

Granger, Mark 2 in green. Underglaze factory mark. 1922-1938.

Granger, Mark 3 in black and gold. Overglaze decorating mark. 1922-1938.

William Guérin Marks (W.G.&Co.), 1836 to 1932

Guérin, Mark 1 in green. Underglaze factory mark. 1870s.

William Guérin Marks (W.G.&Co.), 1836 to 1932

Guérin, Mark 2 in green. Underglaze factory mark. 1891-1900.

Guérin, Mark 3 in green. Underglaze factory mark. 1900-1932.

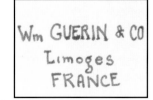

Guérin, Mark 4 in red, blue, green, brown, or gold. Overglaze decorating mark. 1800s-1932.

Haviland Marks, 1886 to after 1949

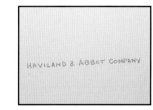

Haviland and Abbot, Mark. Overglaze importing mark. After 1886.

Haviland, Robert, Mark 1. Underglaze factory mark. After 1924.

Haviland, Robert and Le Tanneur, Mark 2. Overglaze decorating mark. 1920s-1948.

Haviland, Robert, Mark 3. Overglaze decorating mark. After 1941.

Haviland, Robert and C. Parlon, Mark 4. Overglaze decorating mark. After 1949.

H&C, Mark. Underglaze factory mark. 1880s-1891.

Below left:
Haviland & Cie marks. *Courtesy of Haviland Collectors Internationale Foundation.*

Below right:
Frank and Theodore Haviland marks and dates. *Courtesy of Haviland Collectors Internationale Foundation.*

Haviland Marks

HAVILAND & CIE. 1842-1931

BLANKS:

Mark A —	HAVILAND *Incised on Tablet*	— 1853
Mark B —	HAVILAND H&Cº *Incised*	— 1865

Underglaze Green Marks

Mark C —	H&Cº	— 1876-1879
Mark D —	H&Cº	— 1876-1886
Mark E —	H&Cº	— 1877
Mark F —	H&Cº / L	— 1876-1889
Mark G —	H&Cº / DEPOSE	— 1887
Mark H —	H&Cº / L / FRANCE	— 1888-1896
Mark I —	Haviland France	— 1894-1931

DECORATOR MARKS:

Varied Colors Overglaze

Mark a —	FABRIQUE PAR HAVILAND & Cº POUR J.W. BOTELER & BRO. WASHINGTON / HAVILAND & Cº LIMOGES	— prior to 1876

Mark b —	H&C	— 1876-1878
Mark c —	HAVILAND & Cº Limoges	— 1876-1878/ 1889-1931
Mark d —	HAVILAND & Cº	— 1879-1883
Mark e —	H&Cº ELITE	— 1878-1883
Mark f —	H&Cº SPECIAL	— 1879-1889
Mark g —	HAVILAND LIMOGES	— 1879-1889
Mark h —	Haviland & Cº Limoges Feu de Four	— 1893-1895
Mark i —	Décoré par HAVILAND & Cº Limoges	— 1905-1930 (America) 1926-1931 (France)

HAVILAND & Co. 1875-1885

Haviland Pottery and Stoneware

Mark V —	H & Cº / L	— 1875-1882
Mark W —	HAVILAND & Cº Limoges	— 1875-1882
Mark X —	H&Cº	— 1883-1885
Mark Y —	H & Cº / L HAVILAND HAVILAND LIMOGES	— 1883-1885

FRANK HAVILAND 1910-1931

BLANKS:

Mark A1 —	FRANK HAVILAND LIMOGES	— 1910-1914
Mark A2 —	Frank Haviland Limoges	— 1914-1925
Mark A3 —	FRANK HAVILAND L B S LIMOGES	— 1925-1931

THÉODORE HAVILAND 1892-1967

BLANKS:

Colors Usually Green Underglaze

Mark J —	TH	— 1892
Mark K —	MONT. MERY FRANCE	— 1892
Mark L —	Théo Haviland Limoges FRANCE	— 1893
Mark M —	T·H	— 1894-1957
Mark N —	THEODORE HAVILAND *Blue*	— 1912
Mark O —	THEODORE HAVILAND	— 1920-1936
Mark P —	LIMOGES THEODORE HAVILAND	— 1936-1945
Mark Q —	Haviland France	— 1946-1962
Mark R —	Haviland France Limoges	— 1962

Mark S —	THEODORE HAVILAND NEW YORK *Green or Black*	— 1936
Mark T —	Theodore Haviland New York MADE IN AMERICA *Red or Black*	— 1937-1956
Mark U —	HAVILAND U.S.A. *Red*	— 1957

DECORATOR MARKS:

Colors Green and/or Red Underglaze

Mark j —	TH *Red*	— probably 1892
Mark k —	Porcelaine Mousseline TH Limoges FRANCE	— 1894
Mark l —	Porcelaine Mousseline T·H Limoges FRANCE	— 1894
Mark m —	Porcelaine Theo. Haviland Limoges FRANCE	— 1895
Mark n —	Porcelaine Theo. Haviland Limoges FRANCE	— 1895
Mark o —	Théodore Haviland Limoges	— 1897
Mark p —	Théodore Haviland Limoges FRANCE	— 1903
Mark q —	Théodore Haviland Limoges FRANCE	— 1903
Mark r —	Théodore Haviland Limoges FRANCE	— 1925
Mark s —	HAVILAND LIMOGES FRANCE	— 1958
Mark t —	Haviland LIMOGES FRANCE	— 1967

A. Klingenberg Marks (AK) / Charles Dwenger Marks (AKCD), 1880s to 1910

Klingenberg, Mark 1 in red. Overglaze decorating mark. Early 1880s.

Klingenberg, Mark 2 in red. Overglaze decorating mark. 1880s-1890s.

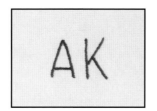

Klingenberg, Mark 3 in green. Impressed or underglaze factory mark. 1880s-1890.

Klingenberg, Mark 4 in green. Underglaze factory mark. After 1891.

Klingenberg, Mark 5 in green. Underglaze factory mark. 1890s.

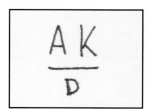

Klingenberg, Mark 6 in green. Underglaze factory mark. 1890s-1910, but after Mark 5.

Klingenberg, Mark 7 in green. Underglaze factory mark. 1890s-1910.

Klingenberg, Mark 8 in green. Underglaze factory mark. 1890s-1910.

Klingenberg, Mark 9 in red. Overglaze decorating mark. 1900-1910.

A. Laternier Marks, 1857 to Present

Lanternier, Mark 1 in red. Overglaze decorating mark. 1890s.

Lanternier, Mark 2 in green. Underglaze factory mark. 1890s.

Lanternier, Mark 3 in green. Underglaze factory mark. 1890s.

Lanternier, Mark 4 in green. Underglaze factory mark. 1891-1914.

Lanternier, Mark 5 in blue. Overglaze exporting or decorating mark. Before 1890.

Lanternier, Mark 6 in red, brown, or blue. Overglaze decorating mark. 1891-1914.

Lanternier, Mark 7 in red and black. Overglaze decorating mark. After World War I.

La Porcelaine Limousine Marks (PL), 1906 to 1938

La Porcelaine Limousine, Mark 1 in green. Underglaze factory mark. 1905-1930s.

La Porcelaine Limousine, Mark 2 in green. Underglaze factory mark. 1905-1930s.

Raymond Laporte Marks, ca. 1883 to 1897

Latrille Frères Marks, 1899 to 1913

La Porcelaine Limousine, Mark 3 in green. Underglaze factory mark. 1905-1930s.

La Porcelaine Limousine, Mark 4 in red. Overglaze decorating mark. 1905-1930s.

Laporte, Raymonde, Mark 1. 1883-1890.

Laporte, Raymond, Mark 2. Overglaze decorating mark. 1891-1897.

Latrille Frères, Mark 1. Underglaze factory mark. 1899-1913.

Latrille Frères, Mark 2. Overglaze decorating mark. 1899-1908, probably toward end of period.

Laviolette Mark, 1896 to 1905

Lazeyras, Rose

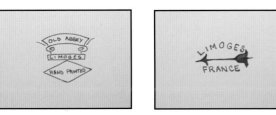

Latrille Frères, Mark 3. Overglaze decorating mark. 1908-1913.

Laviolette, Mark. Underglaze factory mark. 1896-1905.

Lazeyras, Rosenfeld, and Lehman (LR&L), Mark 1 in red or blue. Overglaze decorating mark. 1920s.

Lazeyras, Rosenfeld, and Lehman, Mark 2 in red. Overglaze decorating mark. 1920s.

Lazeyras, Rosenfeld, and Lehman, Mark 3 in gray or green. Overglaze decorating mark. 1920s.

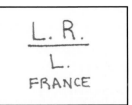

Lazeyras, Rosenfeld, and Lehman, Mark 4 in blue. Overglaze decorating mark. After 1922.

Legrand Mark, 1920s

P. H. Leonard Marks (PHL), 1890s to 1914

L. W. Levy & Co. Marks (IMPERIAL), ca. 1880s to 1920s

Lazeyras, Rosenfeld, and Lehman, Mark 5 in blue. Overglaze decorating mark. After 1922.

Legrand, Mark in green. Underglaze factory mark. 1920s.

Leonard, P.H., Mark 1. Overglaze decorating mark. 1890s-1914.

Leonard, P.H., Mark 2. Overglaze decorating mark. 1890s-1914.

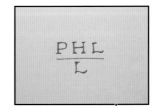

Leonard, P.H., Mark 3. Overglaze exporting mark. 1890s-1914.

Levy, Imperial, Mark 1. Overglaze decorating mark. 1800s-early 1900s.

Limoges France Marks, 1891 and after

Levy, Imperial Limoges France, Mark 2. Overglaze decorating mark. 1800s-early 1900s.

Levy, L.D.C., Limoges France, Mark 3. Overglaze decorating mark. Post World War I-1920s.

Limoges France, Mark 1 in green. Underglaze factory mark. After 1891.

Limoges France, Mark 2 in green. Underglaze factory mark. After 1891.

Limoges France, Mark 3 in green. Underglaze factory mark. After 1891.

Limoges France, Mark 4 in green. Underglaze factory mark. After 1891.

Limoges France, Mark 5 in green. Underglaze factory mark. After 1891.

Limoges France, Mark 6 in green. Underglaze factory mark. After 1891.

Limoges France, Mark 7 in green. Underglaze factory mark. After 1891.

Limoges France, Mark 8 in blue. Overglaze decorating or exporting mark. After 1891.

Limoges France, Mark 9 in gray. Overglaze decorating mark. After 1908.

Limoges Castel, Mark. Underglaze factory mark. 1955-1979

Charles Martin Marks, 1880s to 1935

P.M. Mavaleix Mark, 1908 to 1914

J. Mc. D. & S. Marks, 1880s to 1914

Martin, Mark 1 in green. Underglaze factory mark. After 1891.

Martin, Mark 2 in green. Underglaze factory mark. Early 1900s-1930s.

Martin, Mark 3 in blue or green. Overglaze decorating mark. Early 1900s-mid 1930s.

Mavaleix, Mark in green. Underglaze factory mark. 1908-1914.

MC.D.&S., J., Mark 1. Overglaze decorating mark. 1880s-1890.

MC.D.&S., J., Mark 2. Overglaze decorating mark. 1890-1914.

P. Merlin-Lemas Marks (PML), 1920s

Merlin-Lemas, P. (PML), Mark 1. Underglaze factory mark. 1920s.

Merlin-Lemas., P., Mark 2. Overglaze decorating mark. 1920s.

Pairpoint Mark, 1880s to 1900

Pairpoint, Mark in green. Overglaze decorating mark for American decorating factory. 1880s.

Paroutaud Freres Marks, 1902 to 1916

Paroutaud Freres, Mark 1 in green. Underglaze factory mark. 1903-1917.

Paroutaud Freres, Mark 2 in green. Underglaze factory mark. 1903-1917.

A. Pillivuyt Mark, 1913 to 1936

Pillivuyt, A., Mark. 1920s.

Pitkin & Brooks Mark, 1872 to 1938

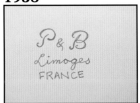

Pitkin & Brooks, Mark. Overglaze import and decorating mark. 1872-1938.

Plainemaison Mark, 1890s to 1910

Plainemaison, Mark 1 in green. Underglaze factory mark. 1890s-1910.

Porcelaine Pallas Mark, 1926 to 1950

Porcelaine Pallas, Mark. Overglaze decorating mark in green. 1926-1950.

Jean Pouyat Marks (JP), 1832 to 1932

Pouyat, Jean, Mark 1 in green. Underglaze factory mark. 1850s-1875.

Pouyat, Jean, Mark 2 in red. Overglaze decorating mark. 1850s-1875.

Pouyat, Jean, Mark 3 in green. Underglaze factory mark. After 1876-1890.

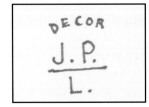

Pouyat, Jean, Mark 4 in red. Overglaze decorating mark. 1876-1890.

Pouyat, Jean, Mark 5 in green. Underglaze factory mark. 1891-1932.

Pouyat, Jean, a variation of Mark 5.

Pouyat, Jean, Mark 6 in red. Overglaze decorating mark. After 1890, used for a short time.

Pouyat, Jean, Mark 7 in red. Overglaze decorating mark. 1890s-1914.

Pouyat, Jean, Mark 8 in green. Overglaze decorating mark. 1914-1932.

Raynaud Marks, 1920s to 1930s

Martial Redon Marks (MR), 1882 to 1896

Pouyat, Jean, Mark 9, in green and pink. Overglaze decorating mark. 1914-1932.

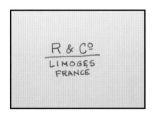

Raynaud, M. (R&Co.), Mark 1. Underglaze factory mark. 1920s-1930s.

Raynaud, M. (R&Co.), Mark 2. Overglaze decorating mark. 1920s-1930s.

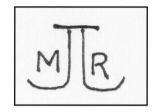

Redon, M., Mark 1 in green. Underglaze factory mark. 1882-1890.

Redon, M., Mark 2 in green. Underglaze factory mark. 1891-1896.

Redon, M., Mark 2a in green. Underglaze factory mark with the word "Limoges."

Leon Sazerat and Blondeau Marks (LS), 1880s to 1891

Royal China Mark, 1900s to 1920s

Redon, M., Mark 3 in red or blue. Overglaze decorating mark. 1882-1896.

Redon, M., Mark 4 in red. Overglaze decorating mark. 1882-1896.

Redon, M., Barny & Rigoni, Mark. 1902-1904.

Royal China, Mark. Overglaze decorating mark. After 1922.

Sazerat, L., Mark 1. Underglaze factory mark. Before 1891.

Sazerat, L., Mark 2. Overglaze decorating mark. Before 1891.

Charles Serpaut Mark, 1920s to 1930s

Lewis Straus and Sons Marks (L.S.&S.), 1890s to 1920s

Teissonniere, Jules Marks, 1908 to 1940s

Leon Texeraud Marks, 1920s

Sazerat, L., Mark 3. Overglaze decorating mark. After 1891-late 1890s.

Serpaut, Charles, Mark. Underglaze factory mark. 1920s-1930s.

Straus, Lewis and Sons, Mark in green, blue, red, or gray. Overglaze exporting mark. 1890s-1920.

Teissonniere, Jules, Mark 1. 1908-1940s.

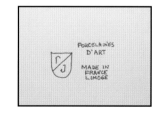

Teissonniere, Jules, Mark 2. 1908-1940s.

Texeraud, Leon, Mark 1. 1920s.

Camille Tharaud Marks (CT), 1920s to late 1960s

Touze, Lemaitre Freres & Blancher Marks (T. L. B.), 1920s to 1930s

Tressemann & Vogt Marks (T&V), 1880s to 1907

Texeraud, Leon, Mark 2. 1920s.

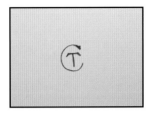

Tharaud, C., Mark 1. 1920s.

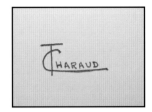

Tharaud, Mark 2. 1920s.

Touze, Lemaitre Freres, & Blancher, Mark 1. 1920s.

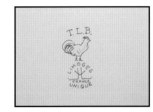

Touze, Lemaitre Freres, & Blancher, Mark 2. 1920s.

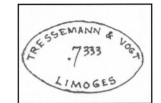

Tressemann & Vogt, Mark 1 in blue. Overglaze exporting mark. 1880s-1891.

Tressemann & Vogt, Mark 2 in purple, red, or gold. Overglaze decorating mark. Early 1880s.

Tressemann & Vogt, Mark 3 in brown. Overglaze decorating mark. After 1891, very rare.

Tressemann & Vogt, Mark 4a, in green. Underglaze factory mark. Early 1890s.

Tressemann & Vogt, Mark 4b, in green. Underglaze factory mark. 1892-1907 but before Mark 5a.

Tressemann & Vogt, Mark 5a in green. Underglaze factory mark. 1892-1907.

Tressemann & Vogt, Mark 5b in green. Underglaze factory mark. This mark is found on items decorated with famous people or commemorative events.

Tressemann & Vogt, Mark 6 in green. Underglaze factory mark. 1892-1907, around 1900s.

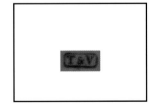

Tressemann & Vogt, Mark 7 in green. Underglaze factory mark. 1892-1907, later part of period.

Variation of Tressemann & Vogt, Mark 7 in green. Underglaze factory mark. 1892-1907, later part of period.

Tressemann & Vogt, Mark 8 in green. Underglaze factory mark. 1907-1919.

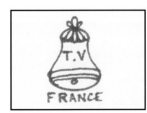

Tressemann & Vogt, Mark 9 in purple. Overglaze decorating mark. 1892-1907, early part of period.

Tressemann & Vogt, Mark 10 in red or gold. Overglaze decorating mark. 1892-1907, about 1900.

Tressemann & Vogt, Mark 11 in red, brown, or gold. Overglaze decorating mark. 1892-1907, latter part of period.

Tressemann & Vogt, Mark 12 in purple. Overglaze decorating mark. 1907-1919, very rare.

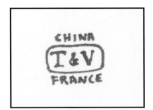

Tressemann & Vogt, Mark 13 in red. Overglaze decorating mark. 1907-1919, very rare.

Tressemann & Vogt, Mark 14 in green. Overglaze decorating mark. 1907-1919, very rare.

Tressemann & Vogt, Mark 15 in purple. Overglaze decorating mark.

Tressemann & Vogt, Mark 16 in purple. Overglaze decorating mark. 1907-1919.

Union Céramique Marks (UC), 1901-1938

Union Limousine Mark, 1908 to Present

V. F. Mark, Early 1890s

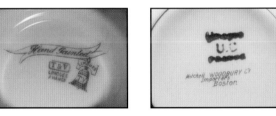

Tressemann & Vogt, Mark 16b, in purple. Overglaze decorating mark, like Mark 16 with addition of banner with "Hand Painted." 1907-1919.

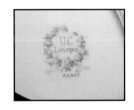

Union Céramique, Mark 1 in green. Underglaze factory mark. 1909-1938.

Union Céramique, Mark 2 in red. Overglaze decorating mark. 1909-1938.

Union Céramique, Mark 3. 1901-1938.

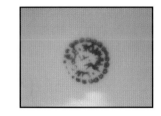

Union Limousine, Mark. Underglaze factory mark. 1930s-1950s.

V.F., Mark 1 in green. Underglaze factory mark. Early 1890s.

Vignaud Frères Marks, 1911 to 1970

Vultury Freres Mark, 1887 to 1904

Wanamaker's Mark, 1900

Vignaud Frères, Mark 1 in green. Underglaze factory mark. After 1911-1938.

Vignaud Frères, Mark 2 in green. Overglaze decorating mark. 1911-1938.

Vignaud Frères, Mark 3 in green. Underglaze factory mark. 1938 and after.

Vultury Freres, Mark. Underglaze factory mark. 1887-1904.

Wanamaker's, Mark in green. Overglaze importing mark. Early 1900s.

American Limoges Factory Marks

The artist renditions shown here of American Limoges factory marks are included to assist collectors in distinguishing American Limoges—an earthenware product produced in the United States from 1897-1957— from the hard paste porcelain produced in the Limoges region of France. For further research on American Limoges, see Raymonde Limoges's *American Limoges*.

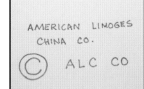

The Limoges China Co.
SEBRING, OHIO
UNDERGLAZE
Ripple Edge Design
& Process
PAT. APPLIED FOR

AMERICAN LIMOGES
CHINA CO.

© ALC CO

Guild Edge

peach-blo

PEACH-BLO
by
Limoges
SEBRING
OHIO

Ideal
IMI3.

Glo Pêche
WARE
by
Limoges
SEBRING,
OHIO.

peach-blo ware
by
Limoges
Sebring Ohio

PEACH-BLO
WARE
by
Limoges
SEBRING,
OHIO.

TRADE MARK REG. SER. N° 283497
SILVER MOON 4M132

peach-blo
by
Limoges
SEBRING OHIO

Ritz Platinum

CANDLE + LIGHT
by
AMERICAN
LIMOGES
CHINA·CO·SEBRING

CANDLE + LIGHT
MADE IN U.S.A.
LIMOGES
WARRANTED
22 K. GOLD

Guaranteed by
Good Housekeeping

CANDLE + LIGHT
AMERICAN
LIMOGES
WARRANTED
22 · K · GOLD

PEARL IVORY
by
Limoges
SEBRING, O.

BLOSSOM TIME
9L133

Shell Pink Ware
by
Limoges China Co.
Sebring, Ohio
Rose Marie 3M133

Shell Pink Ware

CANDLE + LIGHT
AMERICAN
LIMOGES
MADE IN U.S.A.   55
WARRANTED
22 K GOLD

LINCOLN CHINA CO.
BY
AMERICAN
LIMOGES
SEBRING·OHIO
WHITE GOLD
WARRANTED 22·K

THE
LINCOLN CHINA CO
SEBRING,
OHIO
U.S.A.
22 K. GOLD

PEASANTWARE
American Limoges
MADE IN U.S.A.

PEASANTWARE
MADE IN U.S.A.
By
Limoges

WESTWOOD
by Limoges China
W
6-46
SYLVIA

UNION MADE
Jiffy
ware
SEBRING, OHIO U.S.A.

SNOW FLAKE
AMERICAN
LIMOGES
SEBRING·OHIO

Regency
by American
Limoges
SEBRING·OHIO

S. T.
EMBASSY
AMERICAN
LIMOGES
SEBRING·OHIO

CAMEO
by
AMERICAN
LIMOGES
SEBRING·OHIO

AMERICAN
LIMOGES
SEBRING·OHIO
ROSE MARIE

SHEFFIELD
U.S.A.
AMERICAN
LIMOGES
WARRANTED
22·K.GOLD

MANHATTAN
AMERICAN
LIMOGES
SEBRING·OHIO

AMERICAN
LIMOGES
SEBRING·OHIO
JENNY LIND

THE LIMOGES CHINA CO., SEBRING, OHIO
MADE in U.S.A.
LIMOGES

AMERICAN
LIMOGES

AMERICAN
LIMOGES
MADE IN U.S.A.   5
OLD DUTCH 5 TC
M. L. F. E.

MADE IN U.S.A.
LIMOGES
WARRANTED
22·K·GOLD

L' Triomphe
AMERICAN
LIMOGES
MADE IN U.S.A.
TRILLIUM L-T SE30
U.G. FOREST GREEN
WARRANTED 22 K GOLD

TRIUMPH
AMERICAN LIMOGES MADE IN U.S.A.
CHINA D'OR
IT-S 284
WARRANTED
22 K GOLD

TRIUMPH
LIMOGES
LOVE SEAT IT-5280
WARRANTED 22 K GOLD

TRIUMPH
AMERICAN
LIMOGES
BERMUDA-T

TRIUMPH
AMERICAN
LIMOGES
SEBRING-OHIO

MADE IN U.S.A.
LIMOGES
UNDERGLAZE
WILLOW

L. Exquisite
AMERICAN LIMOGES MADE IN U.S.A.
5
TRILLIUM IT-T 5530
WARRANTED 22 K GOLD

DESIGNED BY
ANNE ORR
MADE IN U.S.A.
LIMOGES
CONCORD-TC

BLUE WILLOW
LIMOGES

Made for
EASTERN COLUMBIA
By the
AMERICAN LIMOGES CHINA CO.
SEBRING, OHIO
WARRANTED 22 K GOLD
SUNDALE · IT-S 269

Glamour
By
THE AMERICAN LIMOGES
CHINA CO.
MADE IN U.S.A.
WARRANTED
22 K GOLD

Good Housekeeping
BY AMERICAN
Limoges
WARRANTED 22 K GOLD

TRIUMPH
MADE IN U.S.A.
LIMOGES
3
WHITE GOLD
WARRANTED 22 K
IMPERIAL VICTORIAN-T
MADE FOR FABERWARE

WESTERN ROYAL
BY LIMOGES-SEBRING ASSOCIATES
EASTER LC COTILLION PINK

SEBRING
LIMOGES
ASSOCIATES
WARRANTED 22-K GOLD
GOLDEN TEA ROSE-T

Vanity Fair
Dinner-Ware
MFG. BY AMERICAN
By Limoges
WARRANTED 22-K GOLD

American Homes
Dinner Ware D-47
ORCHARD
AIR-SPUN
YELLOW - LC

VICTORY
22 KARAT GOLD
AMERICAN
LIMOGES
SEBRING-OHIO

Vanity Fair
Dinnerware
MADE IN U.S.A.
Bridal Wreath
WARRANTED 22 K GOLD-C

NEW YORKER
AMERICAN
LIMOGES
SEBRING-OHIO

Elegance
W.C. GRAY
BY
AMERICAN LIMOGES
CHINA CO.
MADE IN U.S.A.
First Quality
T-SSEI-185
GOLD PALLADIUM
WARRANTED
23 Ovington's Fifth Ave.

Glamour
BY
THE AMERICAN LIMOGES
CHINA CO.
60 MADE IN U.S.A.
LYNNWOOD
BY HANS HACKER
DESIGNED EXCLUSIVELY
FOR
AMERICAN LIMOGES

C
AMERICAN LIMOGES
POSEY SHOP C-133
WARRANTED
GOLD PALLADIUM

AMERICAN
LIMOGES
SEBRING-OHIO

11
A PRODUCT OF
FARBER & SHLEVIN INC.
BROOKLYN, N.Y.

LIMOGES CHINA COMPANY
SEBRING, OHIO
RIPPLE EDGE DESIGN & PROCESS
PATENT APPLIED FOR

Common Reproduction Marks

Shown here are artist renditions of reproduction marks seen on the bottom of pieces being sold as "Limoges" or "Limoges China." These marks are *not* from a factory in the Limoges region of France. If you see these marks on a piece that is being sold as "Limoges," you should consider the piece a reproduction.

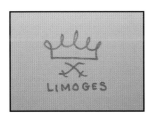

Bibliography

Albis, Jean d', and Celeste Romanet. *La Porcelaine de Limoges*. Paris: Sous le Vent, 1980.

Allon, Janet. *The Business of Bliss, How to Profit from Doing What You Love*. New York, New York: Hearst Books, 1999.

Baker, Lillian. *Baker's Encyclopedia of Hatpins & Hatpin Holders*. Atglen, Pennsylvania: Schiffer Publishing, Ltd., 1998.

Baker, Lillian. *100 Years of Collectible Jewelry*. Paducah, Kentucky: Collector Books, 1989.

Bell, Jeanenne. *Old Jewelry. Second Edition*. Florence, Alabama: Books Americana Inc., 1985.

Cameron, Elisabeth. *Encyclopedia of Pottery and Porcelain: 1800-1960*. New York, New York: Facts on File Publications, 1986.

Celebrating 150 Years of Haviland China: 1842-1992. Haviland Collectors Internationale Foundation, 1992.

Chefetz, Sheila. *Antiques for the Table*. New York: Penguin Books USA, Inc., 1993.

DuBay, Debby. *Living With Limoges*. Atglen, Pennsylvania: Schiffer Publishing, Ltd., 2001.

Ettinger, Roseann. *Popular Jewelry 1840-1940*. Atglen, Pennsylvania: Schiffer Publishing, Ltd., 1997.

Gaston, Mary Frank. *Collector's Encyclopedia of Limoges Porcelain. Second Edition*. Paducah, Kentucky: Collector Books, 1992.

Gaston, Mary Frank. *Collector's Encyclopedia of Limoges Porcelain. Third Edition*. Paducah, Kentucky: Collector Books, 2000.

Hynes, Angela. *The Pleasures of Afternoon Tea*. Los Angeles, California: HP Books, 1987.

Israel, Andrea. *Taking Tea*. New York, New York: Michael Friedman Publishing Group, Inc. 1988.

Jaffe, Deborah. *Victoria*. London: Carlton Books Limited, 2000.

Kamm, Dorothy. *Antique Trader's Comprehensive Guide to American Painted Porcelain*. Norfolk, Virginia: Antique Trader Books, 2000.

Kamm, Dorothy. *American Painted Porcelain: Collector's Identification and Value Guide*. Paducah, Kentucky: Collector Books, 1997; values updated 1999.

Kamm, Dorothy. "American Painted Porcelain Jewelry: Miniature Masterpieces." *Antiques & Collecting Magazine*. Illinois, Lightner Publishing Corporation. April 2000.

King, M. Dalton. *Special Teas*. Philadelphia, Pennsylvania: A Running Press/Kenan Book, 1992.

Kovel, Ralph M., and Terry H. Kovel. *Dictionary of Marks: Pottery and Porcelain*. New York: Crown Publishers, Inc., 1953 and 1972.

Kovel, Ralph, and Terry Kovel. *Kovels' New Dictionary of Marks*. New York: Crown Publishers, Inc., 1986.

Lehner, Lois. *Lehner's Encyclopedia of U.S. Marks on Pottery, Porcelain & Clay*. Paducah, Kentucky: Collector Books, 1988.

Limoges, Raymonde. *American Limoges*. Paducah, Kentucky: Collector Books, 1996.

Manchester, Carole. *French Tea, The Pleasures of the Table*. New York: Hearst Books, 1993.

Moss, Charlotte. *Creating a Room*. New York, New York: Penguin Studio, 1995.

Pearon, Katherine. *Accent on Accessories*. Birmingham, Alabama: Oxmoor House, 1995.

Phillips, Phoebe. *The Collectors' Encyclopedia of ANTIQUES*. London, England: Crown Publishing, 1978.

Revi, Albert Christian. *The Spinning Wheel's Complete Book of Antiques*. New York: Grosset & Dunlap, 1977.

Reed, Alan B. *Collector's Encyclopedia of Pickard China*. Paducah, Kentucky: Collector Books, 1995.

Sandon, Henry. *Coffee Pots and Teapots for the Collector*. New York: Arco Publishing Co., Inc., 1974.

Sommer, Beulah Munshower, and Pearl Dexter. *TEA with Presidential Families*. Scotland, Connecticut: Olde English Tea Company Inc., 1999.

Stewart, Martha. *Living*. December 1994-January 1995.

Strumph, Faye. *Limoges Boxes, A Complete Guide*. Iola, Wisconsin: Krause Publications, 2000.

Travis, Nora. *Haviland China: The Age of Elegance*. Atglen, Pennsylvania: Schiffer Publishing, Ltd., 1997.

Wharton, Edith, and Ogden Codman, Jr. *The Decoration of Houses*. New York, New York: W. W. Norton & Company, Inc., 1998.

Waterbrook-Clyde, Keith, and Thomas Waterbrook-Clyde. *The Decorative Art of Limoges Porcelain and Boxes*. Atglen, Pennsylvania: Schiffer Publishing, Ltd., 1999.

Wynter, Harriet. *An Introduction to European Porcelain*. New York: Thomas Y. Crowell Company, 1972.

Index